Be Anchored.
11-WeekJourneytoAnAnchoredMindset

By

Ariyana LaShae Rimson

Unless otherwise indicated, all Scripture taken from the NEW AMERICAN STANDARD BIBLE ®, Copyright © 1960, 1962, 1963, 1968, 1972, 1975, 1977, 1995 by The Lockman Foundation. Used by permission. www.Lockman.org

ISBN: (print) 979-8-218-38511-8

This edition independently published by Author Ariyana L. Rimson.

Editorial Services by Tracy Crump (tracygeneral@gmail.com) and Gina Johnson (ginaj2250@gmail.com)

Acknowledgments

Special thanks to:

- My mother, Margie—Your stories were the first books I read. You inspire me to write.
- My sweet daughter Zion—You have been so excited to see this book. Thank you for enduring my constant references to anchors.
- Dr. Georgia Pointer and Roz Welch—You constantly push me to write. Thank you for giving me deadlines, resources, phone calls, text messages, and constant encouragement. You two women believed in the book God put in my heart. May this book bring you as much joy as you have brought me.
- My CMLs—You ladies are my cabinet members for life. You hold me accountable to follow the Lord wholeheartedly and encourage the gifts God has placed in me. May this book remind you of your anchor, which is Christ. Proverbs 27:17

Table of Contents

Introduction

The title of this book has a period at the end of it. The
period indicates that a thought, opinion, or statement is
complete. I remember hearing people say "period" when they
wanted to emphasize that they were done talking about a
situation. There is a vast difference between being anchored
and being anxious. The purpose of this book is to help
believers develop an anchored mindset. To achieve this, I will
discuss situations that can alter your state of mind, such as
hardships, sin, and waiting. We will set the foundation for an
anchored state of mind. It begins with a clear understanding of
the gospel of Jesus Christ, coupled with a total dependence on
God's grace.

When people lack a clear understanding of the gospel of
Jesus Christ, they may seek validation and security in people,
places, and things. A lack of security regarding purpose and
place in this world leads to anxiety. We get anxious about our
decisions and how others view us when we don't understand
our purpose.

I have a few questions: How do you react when things are
going just as you planned? And how do you react when things
are out of your control? When things are going as planned, I
feel calm, encouraged, and secure in my abilities. However,

when things are out of my control, anxiety creeps in like a lion coming up on its prey. I have experienced stomach issues, headaches, and frustration. At times, I've even felt like a failure.

If you are like me, you hate to vacillate between these two mindsets: secure and insecure, conquering and defeated, anchored and anxious. I will be completely vulnerable with you. I have bargained with God to answer my prayer requests, cried, yelled at God, slept, not slept, overeaten, and refused food. One early morning during my devotion time, I was fed up with myself. Have you ever been there? Have you ever told yourself to get it together? I told the Lord I was tired of being shaken. Whenever something difficult arose, I began to doubt the Lord's goodness and power. Instead of trusting God and consulting Him first, I reached out to others or relied on my strength to make it through. Of course, I ended up praying and reading the Word of God. I even had vital Scripture passages to refer to, but it took me a while to get to that point. Then, the Lord started to impress the symbol of an anchor on my heart. Hebrews 6:19 quickly became a foundational verse because of the connection between an anchor and the soul. I recognized that my soul was the part of me that needed to be anchored and secure in Christ.

My prayer for all who read this book is that they may grasp hold of our Anchor, who is Christ Jesus. There is no other hope but Jesus. "This hope we have as an anchor for the soul, a hope both sure and steadfast and one which enters within the veil" (Hebrews 6:19).

Our hope is not in what could or should happen but in what has happened. Christ has come and is seated at the right hand of God. His job now is to continually intercede for those who want to reach the Father through Him (Hebrews 7:25, paraphrased).

1

Why Do We Need an Anchor?

When Paul boarded the ship heading for Rome, he didn't know what to expect on the trip. Before long, a massive south wind arose, and they had to weigh anchor. The waters became treacherous as they continued to sail due to the violent wind known as the Euraquilo. During this journey, they had to let down the sea anchor used when heavy weather was present. Many of the men aboard the ship became anxious and believed all hope was lost. But Paul had been strengthened by an angel of God, who confirmed that he would stand before Caesar. He was told that everyone on the ship would arrive at the appointed destination. Paul had an anchored mindset even though the physical anchors on the ship weren't preventing them from experiencing the storm's impacts. In Acts 27, we read about Paul's great faith amid a physical and mental storm.

Paul was a prisoner, and while transported to Rome, he exemplified an anchored mindset to those on the ship. These men trusted in the ship's anchors to keep them steady during the storm. In contrast, Paul trusted the word spoken to him by God to anchor his mind; we can trust in the Word spoken to us in Scripture.

Object of Our Hope

Imagine with me for a moment that your soul is the ship, the chain is your mind, and the anchor is the object of your hope. Most people in a storm search for an anchor, something or someone who will hold them steady. While on this journey, we must allow faith to lead us, and we must endure with faith. We need Jesus and faith in His finished work on the cross, His ongoing work of mediation, and His promise that we will be with Him, which gives us hope to endure every circumstance. In Hebrews 11:1–2, we see the definition of faith: "Now faith is the assurance of things hoped for, the conviction of things not seen. For by it the men of old gained approval".

When I looked at Hebrews 11:1–2 and Hebrews 6:19, the Lord gave me this vision.

We can try to hold onto people, but you and I know that people will unintentionally fail us. People fail us when we put our hope in them for direction and their constant presence. When they leave or pass away, we feel helpless. We can hope for a stable livelihood and feel secure in our bank accounts, social status, and professional networking abilities, but we cannot plan for the health issues that may arise and cause us to deplete our bank accounts to regain our health. We can let self- pride lead us to depend on our work ethic to sustain us. This thinking leads us to believe that if we work hard, we will always succeed. Self-pride always precedes failure, and Scripture tells us in Proverbs 16:18 that "Pride goes before destruction, And a haughty spirit before stumbling".

Whenever humans trust in themselves, they will do anything to keep up that façade. This could result in lying, cheating, and so on.

Additionally, I found that trusting yourself can be dangerous because guilt sets in when you don't meet the standards you've created. When you fail at anything, you condemn yourself because you were the anchor; your security was in you. When you make yourself the anchor and fail to sustain yourself, all hope seems lost. Sit with that for a second because I had to.

Did you know that the phrase sailors use to indicate it is time to drop the anchor is "let go"? What's a typical statement used by Christians to encourage someone to stop worrying? We tell them to let it go and give it to God. We are instructed in numerous passages to let go, Isaiah 43:18–19 (the prophet advises us to release our hold on the past), Matthew 6:14–15 (teaches us to forgive), and 1 Peter 5:7 (we are told to entrust all our cares to the Lord).

Effective and Ineffective Anchors

An effective anchor requires humility because you must accept that you are not in control of any area of your life or the lives of others. Humility builds on faith. Our faith shows that we trust in Jesus. He is our hope, and we believe that what He has promised will be accomplished even if we don't see it or have evidence of it.

Let's talk about some ineffective anchors, starting with ourselves. Our strength is temporary, and we will eventually become exhausted, which can cause us to lose hope. My strength looks like: praying it away, bargaining with God, becoming angry, or leaning on my understanding, which leads to exhaustion, frustration, anxiety, defeat, and depression.

Let's take a moment and look at Proverbs 3:5–6.

"Trust in the Lord with all your heart and do not lean on your understanding. In all your ways acknowledge Him, And He will make your paths straight"

When you trust people to be your anchor, you become emotionally attached to them. You give them authority and the responsibility to provide security for you. Even in the marriage vows used in America, the woman states I _____ take _____ to be my husband. She does not say I take him to be my anchor. Your spouse can't anchor you or keep you steady in life. The Lord must do that. Now the problem arises when you put all the pressure on yourself because you trust in yourself to make your life work out. Furthermore, the Bible repeatedly tells us not to put our trust in people. One verse that speaks about this is Jeremiah 17:5.

"Thus says the LORD, 'Cursed is the man who trusts in mankind And makes flesh his strength, And whose heart turns away from the Lord"

When you look to a man or woman to answer your problems, deliver you from distress, or give constant support, you are setting yourself up not to trust in the Lord. Trusting in man shows that you doubt the Lord will provide or deliver you. We see this multiple times in the Old Testament when tribes made an alliance with a foreign nation instead of waiting on the Lord to deliver them.

Another critical verse to meditate on is Jeremiah 31:1, "At that time," declares the LORD, "I will be the God of all the families of Israel, and they shall be My people".

Trusting in the Lord

In Proverbs 3:5–6, I want to explain a few key terms: lean, understanding, ways, acknowledge, make, and paths.

Lean means to rest upon, place confidence in, or support oneself. I can't rest upon my ability to make it through suffering, and I can't put my confidence in anyone other than Christ.

Understanding means being discerning and having insight or intelligence. We try to comprehend life's hardships, but we can't seem to make sense of it all. The pandemic of 2020 was a prime example.

Ways are actions or behaviors that have become our default. Your default is what you usually revert to or what you typically do in each situation. For years, I defaulted to not eating and having a short temper when I was stressed out. Now that the Lord has consistently trained me to let go (depending on Christ as my anchor), I can bounce back within minutes or hours. I put Christ in charge of the storm when I take my fears, concerns, and doubts to Him through prayer. There is so much freedom in that.

Acknowledge means to know or discern. We are to acknowledge the Lord when choosing a course of action. Remember, your behaviors are a result of your beliefs. If you believe God will work all things out for your good, as stated in Romans 8:28, your actions will look different. Your emotional and mental state will be different. If you don't believe God is faithful to fulfill His promises, you will be insecure in your

walk with the Lord and in all your decision-making. You will be like the man mentioned in James 1:6–7, "But he must ask in faith without any doubting, for the one who doubts is like the surf of the sea, driven and tossed by the wind. For that man ought not to expect that he will receive anything from the Lord". An anchored mindset gives us security, and we need that in this life of great uncertainty. Trusting in others or ourselves will leave us anxious because we worry about what comes next. Do you often worry about life? That might signify that you don't possess an anchored mindset. In Isaiah 26:3–4, the Word of God tells us, "The steadfast of mind You will
keep in perfect peace, Because he trusts in You. Trust in the Lord forever, For in GOD the LORD, we have an everlasting Rock". If you find yourself anxious and overwhelmed with your current season of life, seek the Lord through faith. Christ is your only Savior and your daily anchor.

As we continue through Proverbs 3:5–6, we come to the last two words we will dissect: "make" and "paths."

Make in this passage refers to being level or straight. The Lord has a plan, and it may seem as if He is taking the long route, but to Him, it is a straight path. Sometimes following God may feel like one of those map apps on our smartphones, which has us making multiple turns to get to a place where we would have chosen one street and one turn. Remember that His ways are not our ways. His thoughts are not our thoughts.

Path used in this passage refers to a path that leads to life or death. The Lord is leading us to eternal life, and we must stay on the path He has set for us. When we follow the path set, we are more apt to depend on our anchor in all situations.

I enjoy going walking and on occasion, jogging. When I do, I choose the same paths because I am familiar with them.

However, there are times when I take a risk and choose a new path to explore. The same is true in our spiritual walk; we are creatures of habit, and we can get very complacent with "doing things the way we have always done them". The problem with this mindset is that we don't give the Holy Spirit the freedom to speak to us and show us a different way to handle a situation. I have seen numerous times in my life that when I surrender my will for His ways, the path that God chooses to handle my situation is vastly different from what I would have chosen.

Examples of People with an Anchored Mindset

Let's pause to examine some individuals mentioned in Hebrews 11 and consider how their faith demonstrated an anchored mindset.

PERSON	PASSAGE	CIRCUMSTANCES	PROOF OF AN ANCHORED MINDSET
Noah	Genesis 6:8 – Genesis 9:29 Hebrews 11:7	God told Noah He would flood the earth and gave Noah a specific task.	Genesis 6:22, "Thus Noah did; according to all that God had commanded him, so he did". Hebrews 11:7 states he did it in reverence to the Lord.
Moses	Exodus 2:14, Deuteronomy 34:10-12 Hebrews 11:23-29	Moses' mother believed God had a specific task for her child. The Lord led Moses to prepare the people for freedom from slavery.	Deuteronomy 34:10-12 tells us that there had not been another prophet like Moses. Hebrews 11:27 confirms that his mother did this because she didn't fear the wrath of the king.

Sarah	Genesis 15 – 18; Genesis 21	God promised Abram and Sarah they would bear children in their old age. Scripture states that she believed in Him who promised.	Hebrews 11:11-12, "She considered Him faithful who had promised".
	Hebrews 11:11 –12		(condensed)
Rahab	Joshua 2	God allowed the people of Jericho to hear about the people of Israel and how He was giving them all the land. Rahab believed in the report about God and put her faith in Him.	Joshua 2:11, "For the LORD your God, He is God in heaven above and on the earth beneath" (condensed).
	Hebrews 11:30-31		

Hopefully, you noticed a trend in the above accounts. Men and women with an anchored mindset achieved this through faith. They initially believed that the One who made the promise was faithful to fulfill it.

Beliefs Precede Behavior

Jesus commands us to ask Him for things through prayer, and we should be obedient to that. Obedience is a by-product of our salvation. Paul speaks of obedience in Philippians 2:12– 13, "So then, my beloved, just as you have always obeyed, not as in my presence only, but now much more in my absence, work out your salvation with fear and trembling; for it is God who is at work in you, both to will and to work for His good pleasure". When John the Baptist begins preparing the way for the Savior, he begins his message by imploring the people to believe that Jesus is the Son of God and to repent of their sins. To accept this truth about Christ, they needed faith, and to repent, they had to be willing to obey God's commands. When we surrender to the Lord, we relinquish control over our lives and submit ourselves to Jesus' leading. We agree to obey Him.

Be Anchored.

Let's quickly look at a few passages to see if God's authority warrants our obedience. I desire to convince you that God has all power in heaven and on earth. Thus, we are called or commanded to obey Him.

GOD THE FATHER	JESUS CHRIST	THE HELPER/HOLY SPIRIT
Jeremiah 10:10 – We serve the true God, living God, and everlasting King.	Matthew 1:21 – Jesus can save people from their sins.	John 16:13 – He is the Spirit of truth; He will speak on behalf of the Son and the Father.
Deuteronomy 32:4 – He is the Rock, perfect, just, faithful, righteous, upright.	Matthew 1:23 – Jesus is entirely God and a human being.	John 16:8 – The Holy Spirit can convict the world concerning sin, righteousness, and judgment.
Deuteronomy 32:39 – No god besides Him puts people to death and gives life, wounds, and heals. God's grip on us is secure.	Matthew 8:3;13-14 – Jesus has power over disease and power to heal through His words. Matthew 8:26, 32 – Jesus has power over storms and power over demons.	Romans 8:26-27 – The Holy Spirit intercedes for us according to the will of God. Ephesians 1:13 – He is the seal of promise, a pledge of our inheritance.
Acts 17:24-26 – He made all things; He does not need anything; He made every nation from one man.	John 11:43 – Jesus has power over death. Matthew 28:18 – All authority was given to Jesus.	Ephesians 4:30 – Paul commands us not to grieve the Holy Spirit of God because He seals us for the day of redemption.

As you read over these passages and what they reveal about God the Father, Jesus, and the Holy Spirit, I pray that you have gained a deeper understanding of the God you serve. We are followers of Christ, but we will still feel lost if we don't know *whom* we follow. We must study who God the Father is, who the Lord Jesus Christ is, and who the helper, called the Holy Spirit, is.

Further Bible Study

Look at the passages below and answer the following question: What does this passage of Scripture teach me about God and myself? Choose one passage of Scripture to anchor you this week.

1. Jeremiah 10:10

2. Matthew 1:21

3. Romans 8:26–27

Reflection Questions

1. Have you placed hope in earthly things?

2. Have you fallen because of pride?

3. Is there an area of your life in which you have been double-minded?

4. In what area of your life do you need to give up control?

2

The Storm

When I received the call from my mother, I feared the worst. My father had been admitted to the hospital for a heart attack earlier that week, and his kidneys began to fail due to massive blockages in his heart. His body was shutting down. As I prepared to leave my job as an athletic trainer, I knew that day would be hard. I called my best friend, Josie, and asked her to meet me there because I feared they would disconnect my father from life support. We arrived at the hospital within minutes of each other. My mother sat in the hallway near the nurse's station with my uncle.

I entered the room where my father was lying on the hospital bed, wearing a white hospital gown with blue and green symbols. We locked eyes. Although he could not speak, I knew what his heart was saying. He told me that he loved me and that I would be okay. As tears ran down his face and mine, I hugged him. That day would be the most challenging day of my life. I let him go and walked over to the set of chairs in front of the window. Josie sat quietly at my side, her presence giving me more comfort than words could. We listened intently to the beeping sounds from the machines monitoring his heart rate, blood pressure, and oxygen levels. The nurse came in and began turning off the devices, and we continued to listen to the sounds. I'm not sure how long we sat there before the nurse returned. I asked if he was still alive because I thought I could still hear the heartbeat. She told us he had passed, and the sounds were from the heart's electrical system. Then the storm hit me. I ran to the nearest bathroom and screamed at the top of my lungs as I looked in the mirror with tears running down my face.

I couldn't comprehend my life without my father. When we finally gathered our composure for the drive home, my seven-year-old cousin was designated to ride home with me so I would not be alone. It began raining as I drove. I couldn't tell if my vision was blurry because of the tears or the rain. The Lord blessed me while driving through that rainstorm. The song "I Told the Storm" By Greg O'Quin and Joyful Noyze played on the radio. The words reminded me that what I was experiencing was a storm. I didn't know at the time that God was going to anchor me in that storm.

Choosing an Anchor

When our souls start to despair and hopelessness surrounds us, we must have an anchor. To ensure we are all on the same page, think of your hardships as a storm and you as the ship. Now you can use your imagination. You may want to be in a canoe or a yacht. The type of anchor you use will determine the longevity of your boat when it encounters a storm. Ships can use one of fifteen types of anchors depending on their needs. An anchor connects a vessel to the seabed or stabilizes it when the seabed isn't accessible to prevent it from drifting due to wind or current.

We are vessels for the Lord as written in 2 Timothy 2:21, "Therefore, if anyone cleanses himself from these things, he will be a vessel for honor, sanctified, useful to the Master, prepared for every good work". You are a fully equipped vessel because of the Holy Spirit's power that enables you to endure storms with the Lord as your anchor.

He will steady us during the storm. While in the storm, we recognize three things: 1) The storm is out of our control, 2) The storm is beyond our comprehension, and 3) The storm is not manageable with our physical strength. Jesus shows His ability and willingness to be our anchor through the storm.

Jesus and the Storm

A storm is "a disturbance of the atmosphere marked by wind and usually rain, snow, hail, sleet, or thunder and lightning".[1] It is also defined as a "tumultuous outburst".[2] In the story in Luke 8, the twelve disciples and Jesus had set sail on the Sea of Galilee, also known as the Lake of Gennesaret. Others may refer to it as the Sea of Galilee, the largest freshwater lake in Israel, covering an area of approximately 64 square miles. To provide a point of reference, Lake Michigan covers an area of 22,406 square miles. While standing on the shore of the Sea of Galilee, you can see Capernaum, where Jesus began His public ministry.

Many of the twelve disciples were highly skilled fishermen who had encountered countless storms. These men had fished this lake multiple times because of the quality of fish found there, and Jesus had frequently sailed with them. When Jesus

---

[1] Merriam-Webster.(n.d.). *Merriam-Webster.com dictionary*

[2] Merriam-Webster.(n.d.). *Merriam-Webster.com dictionary*

asked them to take Him to the other side of the lake, they encountered possibly the worst storm of their lives.

Sometimes, when we decide to follow Jesus, we endure challenging situations. I willfully accepted the role as the power of attorney for my five-year-old cousin. It felt overwhelming at times to provide for her, work full-time, attend graduate school, and minister to women through speaking engagements. I needed boundaries in my life, so I wrote out my priorities and spent time in prayer and the Word of God. Even with that, the feeling of anxiety remained. The only option that would remove my anxiety was to quit school, parenting, and anything else that was causing stress in my life. My response was similar to the disciples'.

I looked at the storm instead of the Maker of the storm. Instead of giving up, I leaned into Jesus and prayed that He would give me the strength to persevere. By the power of God, I was able to complete graduate school, continue working, and raise Zion.

Have you ever given more authority to the storm than the Maker of the storm? You thought you heard God correctly, and you decided to obey and walk in faith, then bam, a storm slaps you in the face, hits you in the gut, gives you an uppercut, and leaves you feeling as though this storm is going to take you out. I encourage you to lean in and look at what Jesus did when the disciples feared the storm. Matthew, Mark, and Luke each share this story from their viewpoint. I want you to see the different perspectives of this encounter. Which response do you usually exhibit in the storms of life?

Matthew 8:23–27

"When He got into the boat, His disciples followed Him. And behold, there arose a great storm on the sea, so that the boat was being covered with the waves; but Jesus Himself was asleep. And they came to Him and woke Him, saying, 'Save us, Lord; we are perishing!' He said to them, 'Why are you afraid, you men of little faith?" Then He got up and rebuked the winds and the sea, and it became perfectly calm. The men were amazed, and said, 'What kind of a man is this, that even the winds and the sea obey Him?"

Mark 4:35–41

"On that day, when evening came, He said to them, "Let us go over to the other side." Leaving the crowd, they took Him along with them in the boat, just as He was; and other boats were with Him. And there arose a fierce gale of wind, and the waves were breaking over the boat so much that the boat was already filling up. Jesus Himself was in the stern, asleep on the cushion; and they woke Him and said to Him, "Teacher, do You not care that we are perishing?" And He got up and rebuked the wind and said to the sea, "Hush, be still." And the wind died down and it became perfectly calm. And He said to them, "Why are you afraid?" Do you still have no faith?" They became very much afraid and said to one another, "Who then is this, that even the wind and the sea obey Him?"

Luke 8:22–25

"Now on one of those days Jesus and His disciples got into a boat, and He said to them, "Let us go over to the other side of the lake." So they launched out. But as they were sailing along He fell asleep; and a fierce gale of wind descended on the lake, and they began to be swamped and to be in danger. They came to Jesus and woke Him up, saying, "Master, Master, we are perishing!" And He got up and rebuked the wind and the surging waves, and they stopped, and it became calm. And He said to them, "Where is your faith?" They were fearful and amazed, saying to one another, "Who then is this, that He commands even the winds and the water, and they obey Him?"

Read over the three perspectives the disciples had of the storm. Which mindset do you usually tend to experience when in a storm?

1. Save me, Lord; I'm perishing. Are you appealing to the saving ability of Jesus, as the disciples did? They knew that Jesus had the power to preserve them from danger and destruction.

2. Teacher, do you not care? Are you appealing to the compassionate side of Jesus? They knew that Jesus loved people and that love would cause Him to act to protect them.

3. Master, Master, we are perishing. Are you appealing to the teacher/Rabbi side of Jesus? As His students, they wanted to know if He would keep them safe so they could continue to follow Him.

When studying Scripture, we can use the six friends we met in elementary school: Who, What, When, Where, Why, and How?

1. Who was in the boat? 12 disciples and Jesus.

2. What kind of storm occurred? A fierce gale of wind.

3. When did this storm occur? In the evening, at the end of a full day of Jesus teaching parables. It was an ordinary day.

4. Where did this storm occur? Lake Gennesaret, Sea of Galilee. Storms were common on this lake.

5. Why did this storm occur? Unsure of why—it could have been just a meteorological event. Jesus used it to test the disciples' faith.

6. How did the disciples respond to the storm? They woke up Jesus after trying to manage the storm on their own. They called Him Lord, Teacher, and Master. They stated they were perishing.

7. How did Jesus respond to the storm? First, He was asleep. Awakened by the cries of the disciples, He spoke to the storm and rebuked the winds and surging waves.

8. How did Jesus respond to the disciples? He asked them why they were afraid and where their faith was.

9. How did this storm affect the disciples? They had to address the fear that still lived in their hearts. They learned that Jesus was more than a man—He was God in the flesh.

Jesus chose this storm for His disciples, wanting them to see that it takes faith to follow Him. They had to believe they would never perish if they trusted Him, even if the storm seemed to have the power to kill them. Before this storm, the disciples had heard the promise of John 3:16—that whoever believed in Jesus would not perish but receive eternal life. According to *The Student Bible Dictionary*, perish is defined as to be lost or destroyed.3 They looked at this storm and deemed that it had the power to destroy them and destroy Christ because they said we are perishing in each depiction of this story. They didn't think anyone would survive their predicament, so they ran to their last strand of hope, Jesus.

The disciples were hopeless because their faith was gone.

When we fear, we have forgotten the promises of Christ, and we have forgotten the position of Christ. His role is one of authority and power over death and life. He promised to be with us always, so why is He sometimes our last resort instead of our first call?

What question does Jesus ask us when we start to worry, become fearful, or act anxious during our storms? Why are you afraid? Where is your faith?

Let's examine the characteristics of the storm I shared earlier. 1) The storm is out of our control, 2) The storm is beyond our comprehension, and 3) The storm is not manageable with our physical strength.

The difference between a storm and the consequences we experience while in sin is as follows:

In a storm
You can't avoid it.

You had no warning that it was coming.

You can't stop it.

---

[3] *The Student Bible Dictionary: A Complete Learning System to help you understand words, people, places, and events of the Bible*, ed. vols. (Uhrichsville, Ohio: Barbour Pub., 2000), s.v. "Perish.," 181.

In sin

The Lord gives you a way out of the storm (temptation).

1 Corinthians 10:13

"No temptation has overtaken you but such as is common to man; and God is faithful, who will not allow you to be tempted beyond what you are able, but with the temptation will provide the way of escape also, so that you will be able to endure it"

The Lord warns you that your sin will find you out.

Numbers 32:23

"But if you will not do so, behold, you have sinned against the LORD, and be sure your sin will find you out"

The Lord allows you to repent, and He ceases from disciplining you.

Acts 3:19

"Therefore repent and return, so that your sins may be wiped away, in order that times of refreshing may come from the presence of the Lord"

The Lord wants you to confess, not conceal, your sin.

Proverbs 28:13

"He who conceals his transgressions will not prosper, But he who confesses and forsakes them will find compassion"

The Lord wants your heart.

Joel 2:13

"'And rend your heart and not your garments.' Now return to the LORD your God, For He is gracious and compassionate, Slow to anger, abounding in lovingkindness And relenting of evil"

The Storm Called the Pandemic

On July 14, 2020, during the pandemic, we were all facing a crisis. People had contracted COVID-19 from others, and it was spreading like wildfire in the United States of America. Other countries had been able to control it through widespread shutdowns and stringent guidelines. However, America had adopted the mindset of "doing what feels right for you." Each state had the autonomy to decide whether to enforce safe-at-home orders, require the wearing of masks, or close specific nonessential businesses.

I tried to follow all the guidelines as if it were the law, but that didn't give me hope or peace. I tried to watch the news and stay informed about the new developments, but I still felt anxious. I tried to read various sources of information that people referred me to and scroll through multiple posts on Facebook and Instagram, but I had more anxiety than peace. Rather than allowing every news report, Centers for Disease Control (CDC) recommendation, conspiracy theorist, and social media post to distract me, I had to choose someone who would anchor my soul. So, what did I do with my heart and mind during the pandemic? I decided to turn my eyes to God's Word.

I was reminded of what the Lord taught me about fear. Courage doesn't cover fear; faith does. The main goal of my heart during the pandemic was to persevere, and I encouraged others to do the same. In three specific passages, I began rehearsing verses about anxiety and remembering that God commanded me not to be anxious.

In Philippians 4:6, we are commanded not to be anxious about anything, including COVID-19. In 1 Peter 5:7, we are commanded to throw all our anxieties on the Lord because He can handle them and cares about the things that concern us. Lastly, I went to John 16:33, which states, "These things I have spoken to you, so that in Me you may have peace. In the world you have tribulation, but take courage; I have overcome the world".

During the onset of the pandemic, I wrote out this acronym and have shared it with many people since

P – praise: Psalm 150:1–6

E – encouragement: 1 Samuel 30:6

R – rejoice: Philippians 4:4

S – stay the course: 1 Corinthians 15:58

E – every knee will bow: Romans 14:11

V – victory: 1 Corinthians 15:57

E – endurance: Romans 5:3–5

R – redeemed: 1 Peter 1:18–19

E – exalt: Psalm 99:5

One positive aspect of the pandemic was that most people worldwide experienced it at the same time. Typically, when a crisis occurs, it affects only a small group of people, such as a family, community, or nation. COVID-19 affected multiple continents, various socioeconomic groups, and many ethnicities. We all had to choose to persevere through it, make the necessary changes, and keep moving forward. As for me, I prayed like many Christians did that God would heal the land and remove this sickness. But more importantly, I prayed for wisdom to persevere amid hardships.

An Anchored Mindset

An anchored mindset is what Paul was referring to in Philippians 4:10–14. In this passage, he uses the words "learned" and "know" twice. Paul realized that contentment in all circumstances comes from learning how to persevere through various hardships. The process of perseverance is trial, lesson, trial. The pandemic was a trial. One of the lessons is to persevere even when we don't understand everything. Think back to the pandemic. Did you learn to be more content because of it, as Paul was during his trials?

I believe Philippians 4:13 is one of the most misused passages in Christian circles. Many people use it to give them courage for sporting events or confidence to accomplish things they already have the strength and training to do. Paul makes this statement because God has trained him through trials and he seeks to encourage the church in Philippi to remember that, regardless of the circumstances, they can persevere because God will give them the strength to do so.

The world has experienced pandemics before, and we can expect them to recur in the future. The fact that we have diseases that lead to death proves we live in a fallen world, as stated in 2 Corinthians 4:16. Ecclesiastes 1:9 confirms this truth: "That which has been is that which will be, And that which has been done is that which will be done. So there is nothing new under the sun".

Our bodies may be affected by long-COVID symptoms, cancer treatments, diabetes complications, allergic reactions, congenital disabilities, etc. We are responsible for believing that our inner man is being renewed in the trial by the power of the Holy Spirit. We see this truth in Scripture, 2 Corinthians 4:16, "Therefore we do not lose heart, but though our outer man is decaying, yet our inner man is being renewed day by day".

What Our Storms Teach Us

Our storms reveal three things about us: 1) We want to be in control but aren't, 2) We want to make sense of the situation but can't, and 3) We want to manage it alone but can't. If this is true, we must turn to Jesus, who is in control, understands why we are going through this storm, and has the authority to stop our storm. While reading Luke 8:22–25, Matthew 8:23–27, and Mark 4:35–41, we gain insight into the relationship between God and humans. I've listed these below.

What do we learn about Jesus?

1. He was in the boat with the disciples and will be with us in the storm. In our storms (or maybe just in my storms), I continually forget that God said He would never leave us nor forsake us (Hebrews 13:5; Deuteronomy 31:6, 8; Joshua 1:5).
2. He could speak to the storm and calm it. He didn't have to get out of the boat. Jesus said, "Hush, be still" and the storm ceased. It became calm.
3. He contrasted fear with faith. He asked the disciples for a reason for their anxiety.

   a. In Mark's account, Jesus asked if they had faith.

b. In Luke's account, Jesus asked where their faith was.

c. In Matthew's account, Jesus determined they were men of little faith.

In my opinion, fear is the root of anxiety. Jesus addresses the root issue and reveals that fear can cause us to lose faith or lead us to place our faith in an ineffective anchor source rather than in Christ.

What do we learn about ourselves from our storms?

1. We fear when we don't understand something. For example, we may say, "Why won't Jesus keep storms out of my life?"

2. We think God doesn't care. We see this in Mark 4:35–41, which describes the same storm mentioned in Luke 8. The disciples said, "Teacher, do you not care that we are perishing?"

3. We are afraid to wait for the Lord to deliver us. We want deliverance while He wants perseverance.

Writing this study has taught me that the opposite of fear isn't courage. Instead, it is faith. The world tells us that courage fights fear, but the Bible tells us that faith covers fear. Psalm 56:3–4 states, "When I am afraid, I will put my trust in You. In God, whose word I praise, In God I have put my trust; I shall not be afraid. What can *mere* man do to me?" The prophet Isaiah spoke of this same truth in Isaiah 43:1, "But now, thus says the LORD, your Creator, O Jacob, And He who formed you, O Israel, "Do not fear, for I have redeemed you; I have called you by name; you are Mine!". We are children of the Lord through faith; thus, we don't need to fear.

Further Bible Study

Look at the passages below and answer the following question: What does this passage of Scripture teach me about God and myself? Choose one passage of Scripture to anchor you this week.

1. Psalm 27:3–4

2. Psalm 27:13–14

3. Psalm 54:4

4. Psalm 56:3

5. Psalm 91:5–7

6. James 5:14–15

7. Matthew 5:4

8. Romans 12:15

Reflection Questions

1. Think of the last storm in your life. Was it beyond your control, comprehension, and unmanageable by your strength?

2. Were you afraid while in the storm? If yes, why?

3. Have you offended someone with words you spoke while going through your storm? If so, have you asked them to forgive you?

4. Have you used your storm as an excuse not to gather with other believers (attend church)? If so, why?

5. Are you living in anxiety because of your storm? If so, are you praying for God to remove the anxiety?

3
Foundation of an Anchored Mindset

What we believe directly affects our behavior. If you believe that you belong to God and He loves you, you will live with confidence only He can give. If you believe you must perform for the Lord, your life will consist of striving to be a "good Christian/person". You will be disappointed and feel intense shame when you fail.

When I drew the symbol of the fisherman's anchor in preparation for this book, I thought about the Scriptures needed for an anchored mindset. One of those passages is Romans 5:1–5.

To understand the weight of this message, we must know the context. Paul began in Romans 3:21 to discuss how Christ credited righteousness to believers. This righteousness results in vindication for the believer, and he concludes the discourse in Romans 5:21. Paul begins by stating that righteousness comes to us through Christ, and the vessel through which it comes is faith. By the time we get to Romans 5:1–11, we read about the fruits of righteousness and what we can expect to see in our lives because of the righteousness given to us by Jesus Christ.

Now getting to Romans 5:1–5, we will look at some keywords, relate them to being on a boat, and discover the anchor for the believer. Remember, I asked you to imagine that your soul is the ship, the chain is your mind, and the anchor is the object of your hope. Romans 5:1–5 helps set your mind, so it attaches to a secure anchor. First, let's look at some keywords in this passage.

"Therefore, having been justified by faith, we have peace with God through our Lord Jesus Christ, through whom also we have *obtained* our introduction by faith into this grace in which we stand; and we *exult* in hope of the glory of God. And not only this, but we also exult in our tribulations, knowing that tribulation brings about *perseverance*; and perseverance, proven character; and *proven character*, hope; and hope does not disappoint, because the love of God has been poured out within our hearts through the Holy Spirit who was given to us"(emphasis mine).

Another term used in the Romans 5:1–5 that I want to discuss is "justified". Justified is the past tense of the justification process, which means to vindicate. The *Student Bible Dictionary* defines justification as "God's act of declaring and making a repentant person right with Him."4 Pay close attention to the importance of the Holy Spirit's words in conveying this message through Paul.

Now let's look a little more deeply at some of the words I emphasized in these verses.

4 *The Student Bible Dictionary: A Complete Learning System to help you understand words, people, places, and events of the Bible*, ed. vols. (Uhrichsville, Ohio: Barbour Pub., 2000), s.v. "Justification", 138.

Obtained

Obtained shows us what faith has done for us, makes our faith secure, and permits us to hope in Christ. Have you ever attended an event, and the only way you could get in was through the introduction of someone of importance? Christ is our person of importance that introduced us to grace, and now we have direct access to grace. We have fully obtained grace in its entirety. You may have heard grace described as getting what we don't deserve. But has anyone told you what you don't deserve? Well, because of our sin, we don't deserve eternal life, peace with God, spiritual gifts, a community of other followers of Christ. and hope that God will never leave us. Grace has given all of that to us and more. As Paul states in Ephesians 2:4–9 we have been made alive, saved, seated in heavenly places, and raised up because of grace. You are holding all of these gifts securely in your hands because you obtained them through your faith in Christ.

"And without faith it is impossible to please Him, for he who comes to God must believe that He is and that He is a rewarder of those who seek Him" (Hebrews 11:6).

God must first be pleased with us—we become pleasing to God through faith. That faith must first and foremost be in the finished work of Christ, not in our works because we don't please God with our works. Think about this: If your works aren't the same as Christ's, then they are filthy rags in the sight of God (Isaiah 64:6). If you haven't died for the sins of the world, your little acts of service at church, your five Bible studies, your mission trips, or even your life as a missionary are filthy rags in comparison to the works of Christ. He miraculously came down from heaven, lived obediently to His parents, performed many miracles, discipled twelve men, died on the cross, and rose from the grave.

Two-thousand-plus years later, people are still sharing His message. I'm sorry, sister or brother, but neither you nor I will have that impact. Our righteousness is filthy rags. Thus, our only option is faith. Trying to go in any other way proves you believe in entitlement. A person who thinks their works entitle them or pleases God more than having faith in God is genuinely mistaken. Hebrews 11:6 clearly states that God is pleased by faith and faith alone.

Exult

To exult or rejoice is our reaction to this good news. Faith has been triumphant in giving us hope in our tribulations. According to the passage we should exult in our tribulations. The only way we can do that is if we know that God allowed the tribulations in our life and that He has a purpose for them. The worst feeling is to think you have wasted your time. According to James chapter 1, our trials are mini final exams to see where our faith is. The more our faith is tested, the more we learn to endure, and we see how much God has grown us. Reflect on your walk with the Lord ten years ago and the trials or tribulations you faced. At the time, you probably thought I'll never make it through that situation, but you did. You can tell the story of God's power at work in your weakness. One lesson I learned as a parent is that I am raising my child to be an adult, not a child forever. God is our parent, and He is raising us to be mature in our faith. To do that, we must go through tribulations.

Tribulations

Tribulations or sufferings denote what the believer's life entails in different seasons. We all will experience one or more things that cause us great pain, distress, or trouble in our lives. If you haven't experienced anything that has caused you to depend on your anchor in the turbulent waters of life to steady yourself, please pray for it. I have experienced extreme grief from losing loved ones, being diagnosed with a chronic nerve condition, living with chronic pain, and financial stress, which have all caused me to question my faith. I had to ask whom or what I believed in during those times. As you and I observe our life trials, we become aware of the love of God, we become aware of our frailty, and we become aware of the grace and mercy of God. Tribulations and sufferings have a way of opening our spiritual eyes to see God more clearly. He becomes our only hope. Tribulation or sufferings we are so quick to pray away produce character in us. Nothing else will genuinely develop us.

You will see growth in your life through trials because they humble you. You can't humble yourself. Instead, you must allow the tribulation or suffering to cause you to lay down your pride and lift your hands in total surrender to the Lord. When the Word of God says, "Therefore humble yourselves under the mighty hand of God, that He may exalt you at the proper time" (1 Peter 5:6), the word humble should be read as the opposite of pride. To be humble in mind reveals that you recognize your inability to handle or remove the trial or sustain yourself while suffering. The tribulation causes us to persevere.

Perseverance

To persevere means to remain under. According to *The Student Bible Dictionary*, perseverance is "keeping on, not giving up, lasting consistency, endurance".5 While we are persevering with patience, our character is maturing. Our character encompasses our beliefs, which fuel our behaviors. When we

The Student Bible Dictionary: A Complete Learning System to help you understand
5

words, people, places, and events of the Bible, ed. vols. (Uhrichsville, Ohio: Barbour Pub., 2000), s.v. "Perseverance.", 181.

are going through life and a storm hits us, we immediately need an anchor. Something greater than ourselves must hold us steady during the storm. That anchor is hope in Christ.

Proven Character

The words used here are very specific because Paul says, "proven character." Let's define what proven character is, I always define character as who you are when no one is watching. We are usually shocked when we hear a story about someone and we can't believe that they behaved in that way. The reason we respond like that is because we believe that behavior is "out of character for them." The character of a person is defined by their consistent beliefs and behaviors. I remember a time when my daughter was in third grade and her teacher told me that she was bullying other children in the class. I responded emphatically by stating that was not true. I had watched her, and she had been with sitters and other families, and consistently, her character was one of inclusion and not exclusion. The teacher and I had to meet, and it was soon determined that she was not being truthful. Your character is proven when you are tested. This is where the anxious and anchored mindset really comes into play. Regardless of the situation, your character will reveal what your beliefs are, and you will be characterized as anxious or anchored to others.

Lastly, here is the joy of our justification: Because of faith, we are given the Holy Spirit. Jesus Christ asked the Father to send the Holy Spirit, as mentioned in John 14 and John 16.

In Romans 5:1–5, we see our foundation for an anchored mindset. According to *The Complete Anchoring Handbook*, all portable modern anchors have these four parts in common:

flukes, shanks, crowns, and rings.6 I will use this model to describe how the truths in Romans 5:1–5 establish an anchored perspective for our faith.

- Flukes are used to make contact and penetrate the seafloor. In our passage, faith is what interacts with various situations in our lives. Be it trials, tribulations, or temptations, our faith will be tested, and either it will hold us steady, or we will capsize.

- Shanks are used to bury or set the flute in the various seafloors. In our passage, grace is what holds our faith steady. We would not have faith in God or the finished work of Christ if it were not for the grace of God.

- Crowns are used to connect the fluke and shaft. In our passage, we must make a conscious decision to connect the grace of God with our belief in God. We are not doing this on our own. As stated in Ephesians 1:13, we received the message of truth and believed (paraphrased). We must make decisions with our mind that will affect us for eternity. This is where you put your feelings to the side. We believe because of what we know about God. We come to know Him by the hearing and reading of His word. We don't believe or stop believing in God because of how we feel.

- Rings are the part where the chain or cable is attached. In our passage, we must have faith, which attaches us to Christ. Our faith can't attach us to our works as stated in Ephesians 2:9. When we think that we have obtained salvation by our works, we will inevitably boast (paraphrased).

---

[6] Alain Poiraud, "Chapter 3/Anchor Selection," essay, in *The Complete Anchoring Handbook: Stay Put on Any Bottom in Any Weather. (9780071475082)* (Blacklick, Ohio: McGraw-Hill, 2008), 16.

Trials versus Temptations

Christ has given us freedom because of faith. Without Christ, faith does not exist. We know storms come as we are sailing the seas of life, but those storms don't appear in the form of trials alone. Storms also emerge in the form of temptations. Let's take a moment to learn the difference between the two Ts.

Trials come from the Lord. In 1 Peter 1:6–9, you will see that Peter speaks of trials in the lives of the scattered believers due to persecution. The trials they encountered caused distress. We may feel distressed when trials come into our lives. Notice the words Peter uses when describing the time frame of the trials. Paul says, "for a little while," in the *New American Standard Bible* (NASB) version. Now a "little while" may be one week, one month, or a year, but in comparison to eternity, it *is* a little while. We can look back at our most recent trial or tribulation that passed and remember thinking it would never end, but it did.

A *trial* is an opportunity to show our faith, reveal what we believe, and prove that our faith is secure in Christ. The critical part is that God allows these trials to test our faith. Will we fold or stand firm? Trials can come from religious persecution, hardships, suffering, and sickness. The purpose is to strengthen our faith.

Temptations come from Satan, not God, as seen in James 1:13. A temptation is an opportunity to sin and provides proof that we were born in sin. It also reveals what lies in our hearts. God would not tempt us. Thus, we can't say He has made us sin against Him. Instead, we know that our sinful nature has convinced us this sin is who we are. Temptation isn't hardship, suffering, or sickness. Satan tempts us from the desire in our hearts. We give him a list, and he offers us opportunities to carry them out. The purpose is to cause us to disobey the commands of God and lose faith in the authority of God in our lives.

Whether *trials* or *temptations*, the Lord must be your anchor. Either you look to Him for the grace needed to make it through the trial, or you look to Him for the exit from the temptation.

In 2 Corinthians 4:17, we see another reminder that we are not to lose heart during our trials. It states, "For momentary, light affliction is producing for us an eternal weight of glory far beyond all comparison". This trial or tribulation you are enduring is momentary and light. During an affliction, we feel it emotionally, physically, and mentally, but it still has an end date, whether here on earth or when we see Christ Jesus.

Jesus tested the disciples through the storm, and we will be tested. Their reaction was fear and despair, so Christ asked them where their faith was. I ask you the same question. Where is your faith? What is your anchor? Is it Christ, or is it you? Remember, at the beginning of this section, I told you Romans 5:1–5 would show you what the anchor should be for a believer. The answer is *Christ*. Our soul is the ship, life is the water we sail upon where the storms exist, and our minds must believe Christ will steady us during the storm and when things are calm. If Christ is truly our anchor, our faith will be shown to be as pure as gold because the storms of life have tested it.

Further Bible Study

Look at the passages below and answer the following question: What does this passage of Scripture teach me about God and myself? Choose one passage of Scripture to anchor you this week.

1. Jeremiah 17:5

2. Isaiah 31:1

3. Isaiah 26:3–4

Reflection Questions

1. What role will I allow God the Father to play in my life?

2. What role will I allow God the Son to play in my life?

3. What role will I allow God the Holy Spirit to play in my life?

4. Am I currently responding in fear?

5. Am I experiencing a trial or temptation?

6. Am I enduring a trial/tribulation with faith?

7. Am I afraid during my trial/tribulation?

Regarding those questions, Christ is meeting you wherever you are. He wants you to allow Him to be your anchor, the one who steadies you amid the storm. In the following chapters, I will address how Christ is our anchor in every area of life. May the Lord encourage you through my words and passages of Scripture.

4

━━◄XXX►━━

Anchored inthe Gospel

In Philippians 1:27, Paul encourages the believers with these

words: "Only conduct yourselves in a manner worthy of the gospel of Christ, so that whether I come and see you or remain absent, I will hear of you that you are standing firm in one spirit, with one mind striving together for the faith of the gospel".

As women, we are often told how to conduct ourselves. Do you remember wearing a dress as a young girl and being told to "sit like a lady"? It was also common to hear "stand up straight" or "that's not lady-like" in response to something you did. Whether we like it or not, people pay close attention to our behavior. Paul is telling the believers in Philippi to remember who they are in Christ. He told them to believe the gospel and carry themselves in a manner worthy of it.

Let's think about the word "gospel" for a moment. The gospel is not a genre of music, a type of church, or an adjective used to describe a person. The gospel is the good news that came out of a bad situation, similar to sunshine after the storm and rehabilitation after a severe injury. To understand, believe, and appreciate the gospel, we must first know why the gospel was preached.

Romans 5:12 states, "Therefore, just as through one man sin entered into the world, and death through sin, and so death spread to all men, because all sinned". We had sin imputed to us while in the womb of our mothers. David states in Psalm 139:13, "For You formed my inward parts; You wove me in my mother's womb". He recognized that the intricacies of his body had to be made by the hands of God. In Psalm 51:5, when David recounts his sin, he discovers that the root of it lies in him and not in God, "Behold, I was brought forth in iniquity, And in sin my mother conceived me". The *MacArthur Bible Commentary* describes this passage: "David also acknowledged that his sin was not God's fault in any way, nor was it some aberration. Rather, the source of David's sin was a fallen, sinful disposition, i.e., his sin was present at conception."[7]

Also, in Psalm 51:4, he stated, "Against You, You only, I have sinned And done what is evil in Your sight, So that You are justified when You speak And blameless when You judge". In the margin of my Bible, I wrote that sin is treason against God. I said that because sin is man's way of overthrowing God's sovereign rule. We are betraying the ruler and creator of the world when we sin. Other synonyms for treason are disloyalty, treachery, and faithlessness. What if we saw our sin as being as wretched as treason? David recognized that his sin was a direct attack on God. He looked at the will of God and said, "I have a better plan."

---

[7] *The MacArthur Bible Commentary: Unleashing God's Truth, One Verse At A Time* (Nashville, Tennessee: Nelson Reference & Electronic, 2006), 634.

Humanity is implanted at birth with a heart to go against the sovereign rule of God. Therefore, we don't have to teach a child to say no. They exercise the rebellion in their hearts when they say no. Remember, I said earlier that the gospel is good news from a bad situation. Let's look further at the dire circumstances. When we think about sin, we must separate it into subdivisions to fully grasp it. Those subdivisions are as follows: Fall, Identity Change, Corruption, and Rebellion.

Fall

Genesis 3 recounts the talk between the serpent and Eve. Eve believed the lie that she would be like God, knowing good and evil, if she ate the forbidden fruit. In verse 6, you see a new nature that all humanity would inherit. This new nature causes us to look at something that is contrary to God's commands, view it as pleasurable, decide that it will benefit us, consume it entirely, and share it with others. In verses 14–24, we see how the disobedience of Adam and Eve produced corruption in all humanity and the world. This corruption led to death, a death spiritually and physically. Our bodies were given an expiration date.

Identity change

At the beginning of the Bible, we are told that God made man in His image, which makes us image bearers of God. In Genesis 3:22–24, we see an identity change in Adam and Eve. Disobedience separated them from God's gift of eternal life, thus making them enemies of God. John 3:7–12 shows that our two identities—image bearers and enemies of God—put us in a position where we must repent to be given eternal life. In Ephesians chapter 2, we see our new nature as a living being but spiritually dead because of sin. In Ephesians 2:1, the verdict of death was given because of our trespasses and disobedience to the laws of God. God saw us as separated and dead to Him. The guilty plea was put on us, and we were awaiting the final trial for our eternal sentencing. Being dead means we aren't bearing any fruit that has eternal value. Furthermore, we can't abide in Him when we don't belong to Him.

As I mentioned, when we sin, we commit treason against God (Psalm 51). We go against His laws and are lawless, as defined in 1 Timothy 1:8–11. Paul states that the law is for the lawless, rebellious, ungodly, sinners, unholy, and profane. These are words used to define us before we repent of our sins and believe in the finished work of Jesus Christ.

Corruption

Genesis 6:5 states, "Then the Lord saw that the wickedness of man was great on the earth, and that every intent of the thoughts of his heart was only evil continually". We see that God calls all humans corrupted because of sin, and sin had taken root in their hearts, which caused them to be evil continually. Have you ever thought about the effects of sin on the heart and the world? As a social worker, I see firsthand how sin can pull someone down and make them do unthinkable things. When we look at our world, we often want to point out people's sins and say that person is evil, but we are all evil and capable of doing evil things. By God's grace, we don't all act on every evil thought we have.

Stop and thank God for keeping you from acting on every evil thought. Also, ask for forgiveness for the sins you have committed today, whether known or unknown.

Committing sins does not make us a sinner. Instead, it proves we *are* sinners. 1 John 1:8 states, "If we say that we have no sin, we are deceiving ourselves and the truth is not in us".

We have sin in our lives every single day. Thus, we should be asking for forgiveness every single day. (Ouch!)

Rebellion

Another word to use is insurrection, defined as "an act or instance of revolting against civil authority or an established government."8 At the heart of spiritual rebellion is the choice to serve someone other than God, and we know Satan is the only other option. When the heart is corrupted, the mind has selfish thoughts, such as, "I don't want any rules" or "I can do whatever I want to do." We then become slaves and servants to Satan and turn away from the Lord. Many people may think, I'm not a slave or servant to Satan, but in serving yourself, you are taking on the persona of Satan. He wants to serve and please himself and will gladly show you how to imitate him.

This type of thinking leads to rebellion. We see this seed of rebellion in the book of Genesis. Let's look at it again. Genesis 3:6 described how Eve looked at the tree and concluded it was what she needed to be made wise. Choosing to serve another god over the one true God constitutes rebellion. Eve chose to serve the serpent by disobeying the Lord's commands.

In the book of Deuteronomy, we see three different contexts that the Lord uses to describe the rebellion of the people.

Rebellious - Contentiousness

Deuteronomy 9:7 – "Remember, do not forget how you provoked the LORD your God to wrath in the wilderness; from

---

8 "America's Most Trusted Dictionary," Merriam-Webster, accessed February 3, 2024, https://www.merriam-webster.com/.

the day that you left the land of Egypt until you arrived at this place, you have been rebellious against the Lord".

In this passage God is confronting their continual rebellious actions since they left Egypt. The constant complaining and grumbling, discontentment and contentiousness. According to the *Merriam-Webster Dictionary*, contentiousness causes disagreements or arguments.9 Think of parents whose child is constantly arguing with them about every little thing. The hearts of the Israelites were like that. They grumbled and complained about everything. We have the exact nature as the Israelites and can quickly become discontent with God. If not checked, we will begin to serve someone other than God.

Rebellion

Deuteronomy 13:5 – "But that prophet or that dreamer of dreams shall be put to death, because he has counseled rebellion against the LORD your God who brought you from the land of Egypt and redeemed you from the house of slavery, to seduce you from the way in which the LORD your God commanded you to walk. So you shall purge the evil from among you".

In this passage, God is confronting the false prophets who are leading the people to defect from the Lord. Defection means to have a conscious abandonment of allegiance or duty as defined by the *Merriam-Webster Dictionary*. The false prophet had abandoned allegiance to the Lord and wanted others to do the same. One example of this is a friend who is caught in sin and has begun to justify it to the point that they are encouraging you to accept and join in their sin.

---

9 "America's Most Trusted Dictionary," Merriam-Webster, accessed February 3, 2024, https://www.merriam-webster.com/, Contentiousness.

Rebellious - **Stubbornness**

Deuteronomy 31:27 – "For I know your rebellion and your stubbornness; behold, while I am still alive with you today, you have been rebellious against the LORD; how much more, then, after my death?"

In this passage God is using Joshua to confront the mindset of the people of Israel. Rebellion leads to stubbornness and stubbornness brings forth contumacious behavior. Contumacious means to be stubbornly disobedient.10 Think of an employee who is disgruntled and is deliberately the source of strife at work by his unwillingness to do the job as required. The employee begins to show bitterness and convinces others to be bitter and disobedient.

These types of rebellious acts are done when the heart has become bitter toward the law of the Lord. Studying this and thinking about the progression of sin in the lives of the Israelites after they came out of bondage made me stop and pray. It began with one person grumbling about waiting for Moses to return from seeking the Lord, and then other people joined in the grumbling until they decided God could not and would not meet their needs. Shortly after that, they made a golden calf to worship.

Renewed

But by the grace of God, the gospel changes this bad news to a favorable outcome. Let's look at how the gospel changes each of the previously mentioned subdivisions of rebellion.

---

[10] "America's Most Trusted Dictionary," Merriam-Webster, accessed February 3, 2024, https://www.merriam-webster.com/, "Contumacious."

Rebirth

In Colossians 2:12, we read that baptism was given to humanity to symbolize our burial with Christ, and just like He rose, we rise out of the water. Remember I wrote in the fall section that in Genesis 3, our bodies were given an expiration date. Think about how devastating that was for God. He had just created man and woman in His image, and now He had to give them an expiration date. He knew then that they wouldn't be able to imitate Him fully because they would have to die and He wouldn't. Praise God that He had a plan. Our faith in Christ grants us the ability to have eternal life, ensuring that we will never be separated from the Lord like Adam and Eve were.

New Identity

We as humans have three identities that Scripture explains: image bearers, enemies of God, and children of God. When we accept and believe that the death, burial, and resurrection of Christ is true, we are no longer seen as enemies of God but could be adopted by God. To be adopted means that a person is under the care of an appointed guardian. The guardian, unlike foster care, has chosen to provide care for this child. Remember, God chose to save you, He chose to adopt you, He chose to make you His child, and He chose to put His Holy Spirit in you.

In Genesis 2, we are told that God created us in His image. Because of grace and faith, we are not just created in His image but are now His children. We see this truth in John 1:12–13, which explains that we have the right to become children of God because of faith. God chose to adopt us because we accepted His gift through the death, burial, and resurrection of Christ.

Our old nature separated us from God because of sin, but through faith, we are born again. Everyone is not automatically a child of God. Let's establish the truth and stop deceiving people. So often, we hear in Christian circles or in the world that we are all God's children. As I often say, lies and deceit. When you say you are a child of God, you identify yourself intimately with God. You are stating that God is your father, and He knows you just like an earthly father would. The problem with that is that we are not born children of God. Instead, we are created in the image of God. All of humanity can express the various attributes of God, such as creativity, knowledge, love, and anger. We are in awe of music, art, and human abilities. We have those abilities because we were created in the image of a God who is superior in all things. We get to see a glimpse of that in what human beings produce.

The problem comes in when Satan takes what is supposed to imitate God and tempts man to use those skills to imitate him. Musical skills, intellect, and valor are just a few of the skills that Satan seeks for his own glory. God created man to bring honor and glory to Himself, but Satan seeks to pervert and distort everything intended for God's glory. If humanity knew how much they could accomplish by using their skills to bring glory to God, there might be a decrease in the feeling of failure among many people. We live in a perfectionistic society that seeks attention and accolades for what we have done. God desired for us to have one audience, which is Him. As Christians, we should seek to use all our talents and skills to bring glory to God, not ourselves.

Remember what God said about everything He made: It is good! God made our bodies to be good, our thoughts to be good, and our hearts to be good, but sin marred that image, rendering us incapable of producing the good God created us to produce. I must be anchored in the fact that God created me in His image and seek to bring glory to Him with all the talents He gave me. I must be anchored in the truth that as a follower of Christ, I am also a child of God, and my life is not mine but belongs to Him. I must seek each day to follow the leading of my Father. I choose to fight the lies that I am unworthy, unloved, or a mistake because I was chosen to be in the family of God. I have a family with God.

Righteousness

In the section on corruption, I mentioned Genesis 6:5, "Then the LORD saw that the wickedness of man was great on the earth, and that every intent of the thoughts of his heart was only evil continually". The thoughts and the heart are where corruption lives in human beings. Through the resurrection of Christ, we now have the power to take thoughts captive and make them obedient to Christ (2 Corinthians 10:5, paraphrased). Our hearts are the manufacturer of thoughts, which then leads to behaviors.

We have two choices when we think contrary to God's standards. First, we can denounce the thought and choose to obey the standards of God. Second, we can condone the thought and give ourselves the freedom to act on it. If our hearts devise evil, our thoughts and actions will stay evil. When we are saved and the Holy Spirit comes to live in us, a cleansing begins in our hearts.

There is now a battle between the mind and the flesh as seen in Paul's testimony in Romans 7:14–25. Our minds are renewed because of God's righteousness given to us. This renewal happens because of the fulfillment of the promise God made to the prophet Ezekiel, which states, "Moreover, I will give you a new heart and put a new spirit within you; and I will remove the heart of stone from your flesh and give you a heart of flesh. I will put My Spirit within you and cause you to walk in My statutes, and you will be careful to observe My ordinances" (Ezekiel 36:26–27). In Hebrews 8:10, the writer states that this is a part of the new covenant.

Redeemed

I started out by explaining rebellion with three descriptions: 1) to be argumentative, 2) to abandon, and 3) to be stubborn and disobedient. When you realize that you are redeemed, you can now choose not to live in rebellion against the Lord. Psalm 107:2 states, "Let the redeemed of the LORD say so, Whom He has redeemed from the hand of the adversary". Before your redemption, you were bonded to our enemy, Satan. In Psalm 49:7–8, we are told it is costly to redeem the soul of man. "No man can by any means redeem his brother Or give to God a ransom for him—For the redemption of his soul is costly, And he should cease trying forever".

When the Lord redeems your soul, He gives you the Holy Spirit, which gives you the power to avoid rebellion. Instead of being argumentative with the Lord and the authorities the Lord has put in your life, choose to submit. The Holy Spirit gives you the fruit of self-control that aids in teaching you to submit, listen, and act accordingly. Instead of abandoning the Lord, the Holy Spirit teaches you how to abide in Christ. You make your home in His truth while He makes His home in your soul. When you abide in the Lord, He gives you the grace needed to bear fruit for Him, and you see the plans He has for you to succeed because you are working in His power and not your own. Instead of being stubborn and disobedient, you choose to obey the commands of the Lord. In John 14:15, Jesus states, "If you love Me, you will keep My commandments". We know from Scripture that one of Christ's commandments is to love the Lord our God with all our heart, soul, and mind (Matthew 22:37, paraphrased). Next, we are told to love our neighbor as ourselves (Matthew 22:38, paraphrased). When the Lord redeems our souls, we can obey these commandments because the Holy Spirit enables us with the fruit of love. If you are having difficulty loving others or the Lord, you may misunderstand the redemption you have experienced.

Further Bible Study

Look at the passages below and answer the following question: What does the Scripture teach me about God and myself? Choose one passage of Scripture to anchor you this week.

1. Romans 5:12

2. Romans 7: 14-25

3. Psalm 51:4

4. Psalm 51:6

Reflection Questions

1. Is there an area of my life where I am stubborn?

2. Have I started grumbling about something?

3. Have I told others about my discontentment with life, and now they are grumbling with me?

4. Have I chosen an idol over God to fulfill my desires?

5. Am I reminding myself I have been reborn, made righteous, and redeemed?

6. Which outcome of the gospel is a current struggle?

5

Anchored in theGrace of God

I'm not sure when it started, but at the beginning of my

prayers, I now say, "Thank you, Lord, for your grace and mercy." I have tried to say something else, not to sound so redundant, but my mind and mouth continually say the same thing. I think it's because I am in awe of the grace of God. After all, I realize how sin affects me and the world and what it cost Christ.

Let's begin with the grace of God in the sacrifice of Christ. I was taught through different teachers and studies that the protevangelium is Genesis 3:15: "And I will put enmity Between you and the woman, And between your seed and her seed; He shall bruise you on the head, And you shall bruise him on the heel". The protevangelium is the first instance in the Bible that alludes to the coming of a redeemer for the people created by God but corrupted by sin. God's creation of us is seen in Genesis 1:26–27, Genesis 2:7, and Genesis 2:21–22. These passages provide clear evidence that God and God alone created us. It also tells us that we have a purpose: to glorify God by showing an image of Him in the world. In the previous chapter, you read about the progression of sin: fall, identity change, corruption, and rebellion.

In Genesis 3:15, we see God's grace shining through the dark clouds of sin and giving hope to humanity. If it weren't for protevangelium, there would be no hope, and in all honesty, the Bible would probably stop with Genesis 3:24. Without the hope of eternal life, Adam and Eve wouldn't have a reason to keep living. I want us to see the grace of God the Father. God's grace is comprised of His attitude, actions, mercy, and kindness as seen in these passages (John 3:16, Romans 5:6–10, Ephesians 2:8-9, Titus 3:4–5). Let's look at these passages together.

John 3:16

"For God so loved the world, that He gave His only begotten Son, that whoever believes in Him shall not perish, but have eternal life"

John 3:16 shows us God's love for the world, which is

filled with people who have sinful natures, are corrupted by sin, and live in rebellion against God. God's love for the world includes every political party, every ethnicity, all nations created by man, and every person with breath in their lungs. Our God doesn't show partiality as stated in Romans 2:11. God judges everyone with the same measure: both the Jew and the Greek, the Democrat and the Republican, the enslaved and the oppressor. God's love for all people is the foundation for giving Jesus, His only begotten Son. Our sin deserves the full wrath of God, which Jesus paid for with His body and experienced in His mind. God displays His grace through this verse, but I will sum it up with two words—eternal life. God's grace is that He gives us eternal life for believing in Him and

His Son. Our faith in God and God's Son pleases the Lord, according to Hebrews 11:6.

Romans 5:6–10

"For while we were still helpless, at the right time Christ died for the ungodly. For one will hardly die for a righteous man; though perhaps for the good man someone would dare even to die. But God demonstrates His own love toward us, in that while we were yet sinners, Christ died for us. Much more then, having now been justified by His blood, we shall be saved from the wrath of God through Him. For if while we were enemies we were reconciled to God through the death of His Son, much more, having been reconciled, we shall be saved by His life".

Romans 5:6–10 shows us that God's grace was right on time for humanity. It states we were enemies, ungodly, sinners, and helpless—that was our identity. If that doesn't cause you to stop and think about who you were and how gracious God was to send His Son for you, then I beg you to check your spiritual pulse. In this passage, we see the phrase "at the right time". God saw the complete depravity of humanity over two thousand years ago and began preparing the way for His Son. God knew that I would need a Bible to read and teachers of the Word of God to show me the Savior, who is Christ. In His preparation, He orchestrated everything you would need to believe Him so you would be without excuse when you stand before Him. Have you completely surrendered to the lordship of Jesus Christ? God has given you the grace to have faith in Him, but that grace will not last forever. At the end of your life on earth, you will have to stand before the God of the universe, and grace will have ended for you.

Ephesians 2:8–9

"For by grace you have been saved through faith; and that not of yourselves, it is the gift of God; not as a result of works, so that no one may boast"

Ephesians 2:8–9 shows us the grace of God to save us and give us a purpose. God, in His love, didn't just grant us salvation. He redeemed us, rescued us, and chose to reenlist us to bring about His plans on earth. To redeem is to buy back as seen in the Old Testament story of Ruth. Satan owned us because of sin; we were his slaves. When we understand the grace that redeemed us, we can freely proclaim that we are redeemed. The grace of God transferred us from this life of darkness to an abundant life with Christ. When people move from darkness to light, they are rescued from eternal separation from God.

I love watching movies about people escaping an oppressor or being set free from captivity. These movies remind me of the grace of God and His character as a deliverer. In the Old Testament, we see the judges who were deliverers for the people of God every time they became enslaved due to sin. These judges/deliverers represented who God was for believers, the people chosen by Him through faith.

Colossians 1:13 states, "For He rescued us from the domain of darkness, and transferred us to the kingdom of His beloved Son".

Titus 3:4–5

"But when the kindness of God our Savior and His love for mankind appeared, He saved us, not on the basis of deeds which we have done in righteousness, but according to His mercy, by the washing of regeneration and renewing by the Holy Spirit"

Titus 3:4–5 reminds us of the three truths. First, Jesus is the kindness and love of God in human form. Second, we are saved because of mercy, not because of deeds we have done. Third, the Holy Spirit cleanses us of our stains from sin and gives us new birth. Think of a newborn baby; the nurse uses water to clean the baby of blood and fluids from birth. The *MacArthur Bible Commentary* explains Titus 3:5 as "salvation brings divine cleansing from sin and the gift of a new, Spirit-generated, Spirit-empowered, and Spirit-protected life as God's children and heirs."[11] We can't miss what the grace of God has given us, the indwelling power of the Holy Spirit. We can't be anchored in our faith without the power of the Holy Spirit.

Francis Chan wrote a book called *Forgotten God*, which gives an excellent description of the Holy Spirit. Have you forgotten God the Holy Spirit? Have you submitted your spirit to Him? Do you listen to the leading of the Holy Spirit? I know many people have a hard time relating to and understanding the role of the Holy Spirit in the life of a believer. We understand the role of the Father and Jesus Christ more than the role of the Holy Spirit. Do you have a clear understanding of the role of the Holy Spirit? If you answered no, I would encourage you to study His purpose and role in the life of believers.

Hebrews 9:27–28 makes it very clear, "And inasmuch as it is appointed for men to die once and after this comes judgment, so Christ also, having been offered once to bear the sins of many, will appear a second time for salvation without

---

[11] *The MacArthur Bible Commentary: Unleashing God's Truth, One Verse At A Time* (Nashville, Tennessee: Nelson Reference & Electronic, 2006), 1825.

reference to sin, to those who eagerly await Him". Have you decided to believe in the Son of God, confessed your sins, and declared that God raised His only begotten Son from the grave so you could have eternal life? If you have done this, it's time to live out your faith daily.

I encourage you not to wait to take advantage of the grace

of God offered to you while you have breath in your lungs. For more direction regarding salvation, look at the appendix on salvation at the end of the book.

Further Bible Study

Look at the passages below and answer the following question: What does this passage of Scripture teach me about God and myself? Choose one passage of Scripture to anchor you this week.

John 14–16

2. Romans 12:6–8

3. 1 Corinthians 12:8–11

4. 2 Corinthians 13:14

5. Galatians 5:22–23

Reflection Questions

1. Have you given Jesus the role of Lord and Savior in your life?

2. How can learning more about the Holy Spirit help you to be anchored with Christ?

3. How have you tangibly experienced the grace of God this month?

4. How would you describe the grace of God to another person?

6

————— ◄◄►►►◄ ———————

Anchored inObedience

Obedience is a learned mindset. We see evidence of this in

obedient person? Most people may think that obedience only applies to children. When my daughter Zion was young, I used this phrase repeatedly with her: "Obedience is doing *what* you're told *when* you're told."

As adults, some people think they are above rules and

believe they are in complete control of everything. They don't submit to any authority, not even a speed limit. Obedience is a process that involves your willingness to comply with and follow commands or orders. You see, the first part of willingness is a will. Your will is where you decide what you do or don't do. Your beliefs always precede your behaviors. According to the *Merriam-Webster Dictionary*, "will" is "the power or control over one's own actions and emotions."[12] As you see in the definition, we have power over our actions. No one makes you do anything, not the devil and not others. You

——————————————

[12] "America's Most Trusted Dictionary," Merriam-Webster, accessed February 3, 2024, https://www.merriam-webster.com/.

get mad because you want to get angry. No one *makes* you angry. You sin because you wanted to sin. Satan didn't *make* you sin.

Think back to Genesis and how Eve and Adam made a choice and carried it out with deliberate action. Eve thought through her desired action of eating the fruit. Genesis 3:5–6 describes the stages from belief to action. First, we start with a conversation that compares truth with a lie. God planted two trees in the Garden: the Tree of Life and the Tree of the Knowledge of Good and Evil. God commanded man not to eat from the tree of the knowledge of good and evil because he would surely die (Genesis 2:17, paraphrased). I noticed a few keywords that show us the progression of sin from Genesis 3:6–7.

Eve	Effect on her thinking
Saw	She did not see the sin but rather the benefit of it
Delighted	It was appealing to her eyes; she began to take pleasure in viewing sin.
Desired	She began to hunger for it.
Considered	She allowed a natural thing to have a spiritual impact on her life.
Took	She could no longer deny the urge, so she took the fruit off the tree and held it in her hand.

Ate	She consumed the fruit; Eve sinned at that moment.
Gave	She led Adam to sin with her; her desire became his demise.

I wanted to go through the progression of sin in Genesis 3 to helpusseethatalieisattherootofdisobedience. Disobeying God begins with us choosing to not believe what He hassaidaboutaspecificbehavior.Weknowfrom Numbers 23:19 that God doesn't lie, which means we are trying to rationalize our disobedience by not believing His words. In the case of Eve, she believed the fruit would make her wise. Adam thought what his wife offered him was good forhim.ScripturestatesinJohn8:44thatthedevil isthefather of lies, and because of that we can expect that he will seek to tempt us with a lie. We see from the passage in Genesis, and wecan sharefromour own livesthatoneofhisgoalsisto get us to disobey God. In John 14:15, Christ tells us, "If you love Me, you will keep My commandments".

To be anchored in obedience, we must first love God. To love HimmeansbelievingeverythingHesaysandcompletely trusting Him. The problem arises when you begin to doubt His love foryou,authorityinyourlife,andauthorityoverthe world.

In the Old Testament, we see His love shown through His patience, protection, and deliverance of His people. In the New Testament, we see His love demonstrated through God sending His Son in the flesh to live, die, and rise again.

Jesus was asked in Matthew 22:36, "Teacher, which is the great commandment in the Law?" Jesus replied by telling him to love God, and love his neighbor. In 1 John 3:16–24, we learn what love is and how we show love.

First, love is sacrifice—this at times entails pain and suffering. When we love God, He will require that we offer ourselves to Him. Not just our time and talents but everything. Also, when we love others, we sacrifice our rights and needs. As followers of Christ, we serve others without expecting them to do the same for us or pay us back.

The world loves like this: "You do, then I'll do." Generosity is one of the best ways to show love to the world. But if we're being honest, we get selfish and fearful that we will be taken advantage of or not be appreciated for what we give, be it our time, talents, or money. But the Scripture states that the love of God doesn't abide in someone who doesn't offer what they have to someone in need. Love is confirmed through serving others.

Secondly, we can show love by giving financially to a

family in need, helping with someone's kids when we already have our own, or giving our time for the benefit of others. Lastly, our love for God is shown through truth and sincerity. We see this in Ezekiel 33:31: "They come to you as people come, and sit before you as My people and hear your words, but they do not do them, for they do the lustful desires expressed by their mouth, and their heart goes after their gain". Also, in Isaiah 29:13: "Then the Lord said, "Because this people draw near with their words
And honor Me with their lip service, But they remove their hearts far from Me, And their reverence for Me consists of tradition learned by rote".

When we love God, we don't do it as a routine by saying with our mouths "I love you, God" but not obeying His commands. That is insincere love. *The MacArthur Bible Commentary* on this passage states "Love for Christ is inseparable from obedience."13

The children of Israel were given commandments in the book of Deuteronomy, and they saw immediate blessings by obeying those commands. However, they didn't know a time was coming when their obedience would lead to eternal life. When God commands humanity to believe in the One He has sent and we do it (1 John 3:23), we experience immediate and eternal blessings. Many don't obey His commands, and they don't receive His eternal blessings. Luke 2:52 tells us how Jesus' obedience granted Him favor with God and people. Obedience is a learned behavior, and if Jesus could do it, we can, too. As stated in *The Student Bible Dictionary*, the definition of obedience is "Believing and doing what God says; living like Him. Obeying God shows our trust in God and His will. It is true freedom of choice."14 The desire to follow Christ will cost us. Obeying the decrees and standards read in the Bible is a daily task of the follower of Christ. Every day I must take what I have heard or read in the Word of God and decide to trust it, submit to it, and surrender my mind and body to it. Trusting, submitting, and surrendering is difficult because of our flesh. I can probably love others on a good day but constantly obeying the Word of God takes diligence.

How do we obey practically? Read John 2:7–9 before you go on. The servants in that passage were obedient and didn't

---

13 *The MacArthur Bible Commentary: Unleashing God's Truth, One Verse At A Time* (Nashville, Tennessee: Nelson Reference & Electronic, 2006), 1404.
14 1. *The Student Bible Dictionary: A Complete Learning System to help you understand words, people, places, and events of the Bible*, ed. vols. (Uhrichsville, Ohio: Barbour Pub., 2000), s.v. "Obedience.," 167.

ask questions. Instead, they moved and filled the vessels to the brim. Obey to the brim! Obedience + the power of God = great possibilities.

Submission is crucial while discipling followers of Christ. We must be diligent about giving the Word of God and praying they will trust it, submit to it, and surrender their lives to follow it. We don't get angry or condemn them because, hopefully, we know and share how hard it is to obey.

In the last days when Christ comes back, they will have the Word to judge them, not you. Praise God for the Holy Spirit, who helps us to obey.

In the New Testament, we read about the *obedience of faith* mentioned in Romans 1:5 and Romans 16:25-27. Both passages teach us that our faith leads us to obedience to God's will, rather than our own will. Our faith is in the Word of God, who became flesh and dwelt among us, who died and rose again from the grave, and who is currently sitting on the right-hand side of God the Father (John 1:14, 1 Corinthians 15:3–4, Hebrews 8:1, paraphrased). Our obedience is entirely dependent on our faith in God the Father, God the Son, and God the Holy Spirit. If we don't fully believe they exist and have authority, we will wrestle with obeying them.

Further Bible Study

Look at the passages below and answer the following question: What does this passage of Scripture teach me about God and myself? Choose one passage of Scripture to anchor you this week.

1. Genesis 26:4–5

2. Leviticus 18:4–5

3. Deuteronomy 5:32 – 33

4. Deuteronomy 30:16

5. Psalm 112:1

6. Luke 6:46

7. Luke 11:28

John 14:15

9. Hebrews 5:8–9

Reflection Questions

1. What was the last thing God told you to do? Forgive someone, ask for forgiveness, repent of your sin, etc.

2. Have you obeyed, or are you avoiding the task?

3. Why did you obey or not obey?

4. Do you obey because God loves you or to gain His love?

7

Anchored InSuffering

In Hebrews 5:8, we read that Jesus learned obedience from

the things He suffered. As we see through Jesus' life, obedience and suffering go together. This is an important lesson because there are times when God will call us to suffer as He did Christ.

In 2015, I began having the most severe pain I've ever experienced in my life. A sharp, shooting pain radiated from my left ear to my jaw, cheek, and forehead. It would only hurt on the left side of my face. This pain inhibited me from eating, drinking, brushing my teeth, wearing earrings, putting on make-up, exercising, talking, sleeping on my left side, and riding in the car. You could say it affected my activities of daily living and decreased my quality of life. I avoided many things because of the pain, like going out to eat with friends and talking on the phone. I tried over-the-counter pain medicine. I tried prescription pain medicine and as a result, couldn't drive because of the side effects. I went to the dentist and had two extractions done. I visited the ear, nose, and throat specialist and was in the process of being scheduled for surgery. I received four CT scans, one of which was the precursor for an invasive surgery. I racked up well over $3,000 of medical debt. The church elders came and prayed over me with anointing oil. People told me after they prayed for me that I was healed, but the pain continued. Some days, I wanted to die because of the pain. I tried changing my diet and still had pain. It was indeed a thorn-in-the-flesh experience.

In 2 Corinthians 12:7–10, we read of Paul's experience of praying for God to remove a significant discomfort in his life. Read the passage below:

"Because of the surpassing greatness of the revelations, for this reason, to keep me from exalting myself, there was given me a thorn in the flesh, a messenger of Satan to torment me—to keep me from exalting myself! Concerning this, I implored the Lord three times that it might leave me. And He has said to me, "My grace is sufficient for you, for power is perfected in weakness." Most gladly, therefore, I will rather boast about my weaknesses, so that the power of Christ may dwell in me. Therefore, I am well content with weaknesses, with insults, with distresses, with persecutions, with difficulties, for Christ's sake; for when I am weak, then I am strong"

During that first year of pain, this passage became a pillar that I leaned on while standing on Christ. I knew God had allowed this trial in my life, but I thought I could pray my way out of it. My hope was in Christ. However, honestly, I also hoped in the doctors, the medicine, my prayers, and the prayers of others. I learned after four years that only God can remove the thorn in our flesh. There are times He allows us to remain in a trial until He relieves us of it. We pray during the trial for perseverance while still asking for God's healing.

On July 4, 2015, the pain was so intense that my supervisor instructed me to go to the emergency room. I quickly drove to the nearest hospital. I saw the grace of God while I was there. The attending doctor saw the grimace on my face from the pain, put gloves on, and touched the inside of my cheek on the left side, sending piercing pain through my face. He told me what I had wanted to hear for four months—a diagnosis. I was diagnosed with trigeminal neuralgia, which labeled my pain and confirmed that I wasn't crazy or making up things. That day, the healing process began. The first part of healing involved mental rest because I knew what was causing my pain. I didn't have to try different things but rather tell doctors my diagnosis and listen to their suggestions. Next, I embarked on a spiritual healing journey, which spanned many years. I began praying for grace to accomplish specific daily tasks, and my faith grew because God answered them. I had moments of grace where the pain subsided. One of my journal entries from July 9, 2015, reads:

Last night was rough because I have all these hopes, and then they don't become realized. It's hard when you have high expectations that aren't met at times. It makes you want to doubt God and His goodness, but God's promises are still true even if the circumstances don't line up.

I remember struggling with doubt a lot during this time and the years that followed. I wrestled with the meaning of prayer and God's will. But God, in His grace and love, showed me that all things work together for my good. If I hadn't had this pain, I would not have known how important it is to hope in Christ. Not just believe in Him, teach about Him, and pray to Him but intentionally hope in Him.

During one of the most painful episodes, my neurologist felt we had come to the end of the road with pharmaceutical remedies, and he suggested surgery. I began researching surgeries and found a support group on Facebook. One woman stood out to me, and I contacted her directly. She was the first person I spoke with who had the same issue as I did and was an African American woman. She had the highly recommended surgery and was a believer in Jesus Christ. She spoke honestly and encouraged me to pray hard before choosing surgery. Her pain did not completely subside, and she had some complications after the operation.

I prayed fervently, but the pain was so intense that I scheduled a consultation appointment. I arrived at the neurology clinic with a heart and mind full of hope about this doctor and surgery. God, however, had another plan. The receptionist stated that my appointment had been canceled, and they had tried to call me. The doctor had a family emergency, and they couldn't reschedule my appointment until he cleared it. I walked out disappointed, scared, and confused. I was disappointed because I felt like all my hope was gone. I was scared because I thought I would have to live with this pain for the rest of my life. And I was confused because it seemed as though God didn't want me to have relief.

The Lord again taught me to trust solely in Him and not in His abilities to use medicine or surgeries to heal me. In 2 Corinthians 12:9, Paul says, "And He has said to me, "My grace is sufficient for you, for power is perfected in weakness." Most gladly, therefore, I will rather boast about my weaknesses, so that the power of Christ may dwell in me".

When I look at this passage as I have hundreds of times before and something new jumps out at me, I say it is the illuminating power of the Holy Spirit. The word "sufficient" is an adjective meaning enough or adequate. The Lord was saying that His grace, which is His favor, bestows good things on me that I don't deserve. The favor of the Lord is worth more than being healed. To say I still have the favor of God even though He slays me with this pain is a mysterious dichotomy. To believe that God is still good even though He is not answering our prayers is the foundation of hope. Hope doesn't have a timeline and thus, can't be disappointed because it continues regardless of the circumstances.

In Romans 4:18–21, Paul tells us about this kind of hope that Abraham had.

"In hope against hope he believed, so that he might become a

father of many nations according to that which had been spoken, "SO SHALL YOUR DESCENDANTS BE." Without becoming weak in faith he contemplated his own body, now as good as dead since he was about a hundred years old, and the deadness of Sarah's womb; yet, with respect to the promise of God, he did not waver in unbelief but grew strong in faith, giving glory to God, and being fully assured that what God had promised, He was able also to perform"

God, at this point, hadn't promised to heal me, but His Word promised me grace, His presence, His peace, and His wisdom. I had to believe God had amply supplied me to handle this hardship. In 2018, I started reading Paul E. Miller's book *A Praying Life*, which has opened my mind regarding prayer. In the book, he describes four ways the world approaches hope. We want to have our hopes fulfilled quickly. If they are not, we live in one of four mindsets. The mindset that resonated with me the most was desert.15

There is a large gap between my hope and reality in the desert. This gap exists because I don't see the purpose in hoping due to the severity of my situation. In denial, there is a

15 Paul E. Miller, *A Praying Life: Connecting With God In A Distracting World* (Colorado Springs, Colorado: NavPress, 2017), 161-169.

short gap between my hope and reality because I've convinced myself of an unreality. In denial, I refuse to accept what has happened or is happening in my life. In determination, I try to achieve the fulfillment of my hopes, and through my efforts, I try to change my reality. Lastly, in despair, my hope never increases but is parallel to my reality. Thus, I lose hope. One image I use to explain this to others is that we have made our situation a mountain that blocks our view of God. When we don't see God, we forget He has the power to fix this situation.

I must say I went through each of these mindsets. The beginning was denial. I tried to avoid the pain and act as if it wasn't there. But then the pain increased, and I couldn't avoid it. I was determined to make it go away through doctors, suggestions from friends, prayer meetings, and having the elders anoint me with oil and pray over me. You name it, and I probably tried it. I was in total despair and wanted death more than anything. I was like Job in the Bible. Here are two passages that described his feelings, which also resonated with how I felt back then.

Job 3:25–26

"For what I fear comes upon me,
And what I dread befalls me.
I am not at ease, nor am I quiet,
And I am not at rest, but turmoil comes"

Job 6:8–10

"Oh that my request might come to pass,
And that God would grant my longing!
Would that God were willing to crush me,
That He would loose His hand and cut me off!
But it is still my consolation,
And I rejoice in unsparing pain,
That I have not denied the words of the Holy One."

As I sit here thinking and praying about that time, I'm so thankful God didn't answer those prayers, but rather, He allowed me to suffer because it has produced a change in me that would not have happened without that hardship. In Miller's book, he mentions what happens in the desert: "The hardest part of being in the desert is that there is no way out. You don't know when it will end. There is no relief in sight."16

I think of Hagar in Genesis 21:9–21. Read this passage and pay attention to the things God did for Hagar.

- God promised Abraham He would take care of the child. (verses 12–13)

- God heard the cry of the child. (verse 17)

- God spoke to her. (verses 17–18)

- God allowed her to see his provision. (verse 19)

- God showed favor to them. (verse 20)

When we are anchored in Christ, we can live in the desert because we know He is with us, and He hears us. That is where I lived in 2018. I stopped trying to make things happen, stopped living in despair, and instead, decided to live with full hope and complete acceptance of my reality. It was then that I felt joy amid my trials. For three years, I had tried to muster up joy if the pain subsided or decreased, but in 2018, I decided to embrace the pain and hope in Christ.

In Miller's book, he states, "God customizes deserts for each of us."17 My desert wasn't made for my friends, mentors,

---

16 Ibid, 165.
17Ibid, 165.

family, or community. I had to live in it with just Christ, and I had to live out Psalm 121:1–2, which reads, "I will lift up my eyes to the mountains; from where shall my help come? My help comes from the LORD who made heaven and earth".

I wrote this passage on a chalkboard in my house, and it has become my mantra. Jesus lived in a desert, too, while His reality was death on the cross for our sins. He hoped in the joy of His resurrection and reunification with the Father in heaven. I wish I could quote every line from Miller's book, but I must limit it to these three quotes:

"God takes everyone he loves through a desert."

"Desert life sanctifies you."

"You have no idea you are changing. You simply notice after you've been in the desert awhile that you are different."[18]

I saw a change in my prayer life. It became more constant and specific. I also noticed that focused prayer and hope in Christ—instead of hoping in my circumstances to change—encouraged my soul. Many times, over the years, the pain has gone into remission. At one point I thought I was completely healed, but it came back, and I had to remember to be content. As Paul said in Philippians 4:11–12, "Not that I speak from want, for I have learned to be content in whatever circumstances I am. I know how to get along with humble means, and I also know how to live in prosperity; in any and every circumstance I have learned the secret of being filled and going hungry, both of having abundance and suffering need".

Remember, in 2 Corinthians 12:7–10, Paul wrote about his constant request for God to remove the thorn in his flesh. He

---

[18] Ibid, 165-166.

stated he asked three times for it to leave him, but God didn't take it away. Take a moment to think about that, Paul is begging God to take away his storm, but God showed He has something better. It was His grace. I question why God's grace was sufficient for Paul's request. Why was God's grace sufficient for my request? Because our power is perfected through our weaknesses. God saw what Paul didn't communicate. Paul didn't have the strength to keep persevering with the thorn in his flesh, so he kept asking God to remove it. God could give him the power to bear it. So it's ok for you to be weak, unable to bear it, and to acknowledge your weakness. God's grace is the power we need to keep going. Grace meets our reality and gives us hope. Let's look at some passages and see how grace impacts the believer's life in different situations.

Common tribulations	Passage	Man's response	God's response
Enemies	1 Kings 13:1-5	Seeking the favor of God	Deliverance
Afflicted	Proverbs 3:34	Seeking peace with God	Provides mercy
Sin	Ezra 9:5-9	Guilt and shame	Leaves a remnant
Longing for the Lord	Psalm 84:8-11	Longing for heaven	Doesn't leave them

| Wrath of God | Jeremiah 31:1-6 | Fear and despair | Protection |
| Segregation | Acts 15:1-11 | Separate the races | Unites people |

During the initial time of my illness, I had gone to Chicago for a visit and went to my home church. My pastor gave a message on brokenness. He asked, "Do you know why you are broken?" As I read over these notes, I realized God had me hear that message at the right time. He said there are three reasons why we are broken: first for purification, second for preparation, and third for productivity. As I reflect on my season of brokenness, I can see the Lord was doing those three things in my life. Brokenness heals us of pride, and I had so much pride in my physical health. I was rarely sick, had minor pain with cramps, never broke a bone, and could run five miles without a second thought.

The process of purification is described in the Old Testament and referenced in the New Testament. Purification was the process by which an unclean person, according to the Levitical law, could be purified through cleansing so they could enter the sanctuary and attend the festivals. They were granted restoration of all these privileges because they had been purified. I believe God was purifying me of my pride regarding my health. I lived as if I could handle any physical ailment, and God showed me that I don't have control over this body.

The Lord was preparing me to come alongside people with chronic illnesses. It's funny how God allows us to go through trials so we can assist someone else. I have so much compassion now for people who live in constant pain. You don't understand unless you live it. He was also answering a prayer I had as a young believer. I remember working at a camp in Bangor, Michigan, and the theme for the summer was Philippians 3:10: "that I may know Him and the power of His resurrection and the fellowship of His sufferings, being conformed to His death".

God is so amazing to hear the desires of our hearts. I think I was around twenty years old that summer. I wanted to know Christ deeply, so I prayed that I would know Christ as this passage described.

Little did I know that eighteen years later God would

answer it tangibly and allow me to suffer so I could know Him more and be more prepared to help others. Sitting here thinking about the last seven years, I can see that I have been more productive because I realize life is short. I have finished my master's in social work, spent five years raising my cousin Zion, discipled groups of women, spoken at conferences, and written this book. God has allowed me to accomplish many things while enduring intense pain. I think about Jesus, who knew His life on earth would end on a cross, so He spent those three years in ministry being productive, not wallowing in what was to come but working to finish the task given Him.

You can be anchored in your faith while suffering. Don't

let Satan tell you God has forgotten you. God is closer to you because He gives you grace daily to persevere. Suffering makes you take advantage of the time you have.

Further Bible Study

Look at the passages below and answer the following question: What does this passage of Scripture teach me about God and myself? Choose one passage of Scripture to anchor you this week.

1. 1 Peter 1:6

2. 2 Corinthians 4:16–18

3. Psalm 34:18–19

4. John 16:33

Reflection Questions

1. What is your thorn in the flesh? (health, sick children, poverty, family issues, etc.)

2. How is God purifying you through your suffering?

3. What is God preparing you for through your suffering?

4. What are you producing while suffering?

8

Anchored inHumility

I remember waking up on September 8, 2019, at 6 am after a

on my heart to write a chapter about being anchored in humility. Discussing humility was the most challenging chapter for me to write because I struggle with this aspect of my Christian walk. May God encourage you and challenge me to grow in this area.

Take a moment to read Philippians 2:1–18. It begins with a question we should all ask ourselves: What have I gained from being united with Christ?

- Am I encouraged because Christ has chosen to be in a relationship with me?

- Am I comforted by His love?

- Am I in constant fellowship with the Spirit?

- Am I growing in affection and compassion because of being united with Christ?

I don't know about you, but those questions are convicting and eye-opening for me. We could ask ourselves the questions as a self-check and pose them to those we are discipling. It doesn't matter how long you've had a relationship with Jesus Christ. You should see growth in your life because of Whom you are walking with and Who abides in you. At the point of salvation, the Holy Spirit comes to live in us and begins the work of sanctification, which is making us holy. One main characteristic of Christ is humility. Humility is not an option. Instead, it is a foundation for how we interact with Christ, the Church (body of believers), and the world.

I think of a saying in America: "You can catch more flies with honey than with vinegar." Honey is sweet, and vinegar is sour. Humility is the honey, and it makes you approachable while pride is the vinegar that separates you from others.

Philippians 2:2 reads, "make my joy complete by being of the same mind, maintaining the same love, united in spirit, intent on one purpose". Paul urges the church in Philippi to choose community over separation, humility over pride, and peace over hatred. He is already joyful because they have chosen Christ as stated in Philippians 1:3–6.

I thank my God in all my remembrance of you, always

offering prayer with joy in my every prayer for you all, in view of your participation in the gospel from the first day until now. *For I am* confident of this very thing, that He who began a good work in you will perfect it until the day of Christ Jesus.

Paul notices their commitment to the gospel from day one and knows that God will continue to perfect them. In chapter 2, he addresses humility, which believers must address in their personal lives. Starting in verse 2, Paul begins the teaching on humility, and this is the point to lean in close and listen. He is asking them to complete his joy, meaning I am already overjoyed with you because of your salvation, but don't stop there. It's like telling a new believer, "I'm so glad you accepted Christ. Now, let's grow in the grace and knowledge of Christ." You wouldn't give a bike to a child and not teach her how to ride it. So, Paul is teaching them how to seek a humble character now that they are believers. He begins with the mind by saying, "Be of the same mind" (Philippians 2:2, condensed).

In Romans 12:1–2, he instructs the church in Rome to be transformed by renewing their minds. In Acts 2:46, Luke recounts how the new group of believers had a unified mind, which led them to attend the temple daily, break bread together, and fellowship in one another's homes. Reflect on this church in Acts. They were from different cultures, languages, and dispositions. Their differences didn't stop them from joining together to fulfill the task of obeying God's commands. They could put their differences aside because the gospel was more important than that.

Humility begins in your heart but is realized in your mind. It's how you view or think about yourself in relation to God, Christ, and others. To help you with this, I've included some questions. After you answer the question, read the verses listed after the question. I pray the Holy Spirit will speak to you while you sit before the Lord. Try to make time to do this, preferably alone.

- Do I think I am a good person? If so, how do I measure up to God? To Christ? To others? Read Romans 3:11–20, Luke 18:18–19

- Do I think people should be punished for sinning? If so, who does the punishing? Read 1 John 4:18, Romans 8:1, Luke 6:37, John 8:1–11

- Do I think the word "grace" is used too much? If so, when should grace be applied to a person? Read Ephesians 2:8-9, Proverbs 3:34, Romans 5:20–21, Hebrews 4:16, James 4:6

- Do I consider myself a humble person? If so, what is my proof? Read Matthew 23:12, 1 Peter 5:6–7, Matthew 18:4

Were those questions convicting? They were for me. I had to pause a few times and pray. While writing this, I prayed for you as you read it, mainly that the Lord will lead you to repentance as He did for me.

I pray that it was encouraging and challenging for you to reflect on how you think about yourself and others. Now let's look at Philippians 2:3, where Paul states, "Do nothing from selfishness or empty conceit, but with humility of mind regard one another as more important than yourselves". In this passage, Paul again refers to the mind as the warehouse for humility, combining it with our actions. He commands us to watch all our actions and run them through the humility checklist first. We should always regard people as more important than ourselves. When I looked up synonyms in the thesaurus, it was interesting to see the various words used to describe the word "regard." Some of them were respect, look, stare, consider, and concern.

When we think about this passage and consider the command given to us by Paul, we must ask ourselves the following questions:

• Do we show respect to everyone we meet?

• Do we stare and pass judgment on those we see?

• Do we consider ways to bless people?

I hope you took the time to answer and think through those questions. Humility reflects the mind and reveals what is in our hearts. Looking back at the questions, when you intentionally show respect to everyone you meet, you prove that you don't show partiality and that you think everyone is worthy of acknowledgment. If you look at someone's outward appearance, such as their skin color, tattoos, clothes, the kind of car they drive, or the neighborhood they are from, and you inwardly begin to say stereotypical comments about them, you are not showing humility. Would you refuse a gift if someone gave it to you but the wrapping paper was not appealing to your eyes? Probably not because you realize that the gift's worth is not dependent on the wrapping paper. People have wrapping paper, too, and too often, we don't see the gift they could be in our lives because of the package they come in. That is pride, and it doesn't please the Lord.

Humility asks us to be a blessing to those around us,

which includes our enemies. When you consider ways to bless others—even your enemies—you are thinking through ways to encourage them, with the goal being to show them Christ. Luke 23:34 depicts the exchange between Jesus and the crucifiers. While they were casting lots, He was seeking to bless them. He asked the Father to forgive them because they didn't know the full extent of what they were participating in (Luke 23:34, paraphrased).

In Philippians 2:4, we are instructed to be concerned about the welfare of others before our own needs. We do this first by being in a community with others so we can know what their interests are. I consider interests as the things they are concerned about, their prayer requests, their sufferings, their temptations, etc. I'm looking to care for them by helping to bear their load through service and prayer. I can't take on their burdens because that is Christ's job, but I can walk alongside them and be a support for them. It takes humility to be available to people and deny yourself at times. Before you say, "I can't do that" or "I have to exercise boundaries," remember we aren't called to take on the burden for others, but instead to help them carry it. Christ has told us through the writing of the psalmist in Psalm 55:22, "Cast your burden upon the LORD and He will sustain you; He will never allow the righteous to be shaken". Maybe your role is to remind the brethren to cast that burden on the Lord daily through prayer.

In Philippians 2:5, we are instructed to have the same attitude as Christ, characterized by selfless humility. Christ behaved in a way that showed how he thought about us and felt about us. He considered our lives more important than His own. He wanted to be in this earthly life even though it is full of sin. He considered doing life with us and experiencing suffering as a better choice than staying in heaven. Wow! That just hit me in the gut. Christ thought being with us was better than being in heaven with angels worshipping Him night and day. Oh, what a love He has for us.

Humility is the mindset that frees us to obey God fully regardless of what He is asking us to do. Philippians 2:6–11 depicts the attitude of Christ shown through His behavior. He emptied Himself, meaning He gave up His rights to be treated as a king and chose to be treated as a servant. Even as a human, He could have been this awe-inspiring man, but rather He became a humble man that sought to serve others before Himself. His humbleness led to obedience which culminated in

His death on the cross. Remember, humility gives us the attitude to carry out obedience.

Paul is teaching the church in Philippi what attitude Christ had and how His behavior led Him to the cross for our salvation. His obedience granted Him a name that is above every name. Paul talks about the obedience of the believers in Philippi, and he doesn't want them to stop obeying because he left but to keep working until the work is complete. We know that our work isn't complete until we stand before Christ. Continue to have a humble attitude until you stand before Him, serve others until you stand before Him, and continue to be in community with other believers until you stand before Him.

Are you feeling overwhelmed by the notion of humility? If you are, please let me ease your mind with the truth from Philippians 2:13. You are not doing this by your strength because God is working in you so you desire to obey, have the will to obey, and have the strength to obey. If you are anchored in this truth, then there should be some relief when you get to verse 14. You can ask God to empower you to do everything without grumbling or disputing (Philippians 2:14, paraphrased). When we ask God for help, He gives us the power through the Holy Spirit to love others without complaining, to work without complaining, to serve without complaining, to submit without complaining, and to disagree without disputing. When we live like this, God gets the glory. This type of attitude makes us blameless and innocent to the world. We know nonbelievers are watching believers to see how we will respond in different situations.

When I held the role of director for a ministry, we hosted a conference, and I was responsible for managing the volunteers. I had assigned every volunteer to a specific role, and all was going well. Later that evening, I decided to assist with taking out the trash. As I was pushing a cart with trash on it, a volunteer made a snide comment, talking down to me as I served. I remember feeling infuriated because I didn't want to be seen as a servant. I was the leader, and they should have offered to help since they were volunteering. The Lord quickly took hold of my mind and heart and asked me why I was so offended to be called a servant because that is what He came to earth to be. By the grace of God, I didn't complain or dispute with them. I just kept serving because Christ had given me that example to follow.

When we exercise the attitude of humility, we place the

Word of God and the gospel of Jesus Christ on a platter for people to feast on. We offer our acts of service to them from a place of humility. We want them to take and enjoy it in hopes that it will remind them of Christ. Have you ever eaten something or smelled something that brought back a pleasant memory? That is what our service to others should do. One of my good friends always signs her cards to me with the phrase "smell good". She reminds me to be a sweet aroma to others.

Philippians 2:17–18 sums up this section on a humble attitude that begins at the mind and is carried out through our behaviors. Paul states that he rejoices that his continual, unwavering, non-transactional service to them brings him joy and encourages them to do the same for others.

When we think of being anchored in humility, we choose to be humble in every situation. Pride will always be there to tempt you to choose yourself first and disregard the thoughts or needs of others. An anchored believer knows that without humility, pride will take center stage. As I looked up the word "humility" to find similar words, I came to "nonresistance." This word stood out to me because humility, at its core, is not concerned with being heard, seen, or considered. Instead, it seeks not to be resistant. Resistance comes from pride. Pride is like an anchor that will not attach to a seabed and allows the ship to capsize due to the storm. Here is a litmus test to see if you are resistant or nonresistant.

- Do you get angry when corrected? Resistant to criticism

- Do you want others to do things the way you do them? Resistant to other people's ideas

- Do you seek to cut off relationships instead of reconciling? Resistant to unity

- Do you seek revenge with your lack of words (silent treatment)? Resistant to conflict resolution

- Do you get impatient with people? Resistant to waiting

The humility of Christ was shown in how He submitted to the Father, His earthly parents, the laws given to the Jews, and the regulations set up by John the Baptist. Christ could have easily stated that He didn't have to adhere to the law, follow regulations, or obey anyone because He had *all* authority. Instead, He sought to submit in His mind, and then His actions confirmed the humble mindset.

Sometimes, I am guilty of resisting the Holy Spirit's leading, which shows pride, not humility. Years ago, I answered yes to many, if not all, of the questions I asked earlier concerning resistance. I struggled with criticism and accepting another person's ideas and was extremely impatient with people. We may be guilty of portraying humility when it is convenient for us instead of exuding it in every situation. One passage God continually reminds me of is Proverbs 16:18,

"Pride goes before destruction, And a haughty spirit before stumbling". Pride may cause you to be anxious in situations because you want to be perfect. Pride and perfection are twins, and they are birthed out of fear. In 1 Peter 5:5, we are told to be clothed in humility, not wear it as a removable garment. May the Lord help us to clothe ourselves with humility as we strive to be anchored in Christ.

Further Bible Study

Look at the passages below and answer the following question: What does this passage of Scripture teach me about God and myself? Choose one passage of Scripture to anchor you this week.

1. Philippians 1:21

2. 1 Peter 5:6

3. James 4:6

Reflection Questions

1. What did God teach you about humility while reading this chapter?

2. Did God convict you of exercising more pride than humility? If so, write out your prayer of repentance to Him.

3. How will you put humility into practice today?

9

Anchored in theWaiting Room

When was the last time you were in a waiting room?

Maybe you were waiting for your car to get repaired, a doctor's visit, or an interview. From the time we were born, we have spent and will spend time in a waiting room. The question is, what is your mindset while you wait? Are you anxious or aloof, or do you observe your surroundings? One of the best waiting rooms I've seen was at my neurologist's. It had been over a year since I visited, and when I arrived, I noticed the waiting room had been renovated. Sitting at the table to complete the typical paperwork, I looked around the room at the multiple televisions, magazines, windows, and posters on the wall. It was designed to help patients occupy their time while they waited.

Well, I believe the Lord does the same for us. He gives us time to sit in a waiting room between the time of our prayer and His answer. We know He is working on how He will respond to our request. Maybe God is preparing to battle for us spiritually. God may even orchestrate a divine encounter with someone to meet our needs. As in the story of Paul, God may be giving you more grace so you can deal with the situation. He may even be preparing your heart and mind for His denial or approval of your request. We decide what we will do while we wait.

Some common responses are:

1. Walk around anxiously and doubt that God heard us and that He is good.

2. Sit, trying to bargain with God to answer us the way we want Him to.

3. Talk to everyone about our situation and ask them for advice.

4. Read material and prepare our hearts and minds for His answer.

5. Rest our minds by focusing on what God has done in the past.

Remember that the waiting rooms we have all experienced are designed to take our minds off waiting. What would happen if we mentally and emotionally chose not to get anxious in the spiritual waiting room? We present the request to God, thank Him for answering the request, and then focus on other things. We would practice what is described in James 1:6, which is to ask in faith and not doubt that God will give us an answer. The spiritual waiting room will reveal if you are patient, content, and self-controlled. Have you ever seen an impatient person in a waiting room? They constantly ask staff questions, and they may become belligerent.

I remember when my mother became extremely sick, and I had to take her to the emergency room. In the waiting room, a man became very agitated because he had been waiting for over two hours to be seen by the doctor. After my mother was called back to be evaluated by the doctors, I could hear what was happening in the waiting room. The man was going ballistic, screaming at the staff and throwing objects.

Many of us may ask, "What was wrong with that man?" or "They should not have made him wait that long." Regardless of how we feel about the situation, the man showed a lack of self-control. Christians can do the same thing spiritually while we wait on God. We can get angry and yell at God to "do something." We can feel like He has forgotten about us and is taking care of everyone else but us. If you have been in the spiritual waiting room for a long time and need encouragement, take a moment and look at Daniel 10.

In this chapter, the angel told Daniel that he had been fighting since the day Daniel prayed. This passage has always encouraged me because it opened my mind to what happens in the spiritual realm when I am praying and waiting. The Lord wants to answer my prayer and strengthen me through His answer, but Satan wants to fight against God.

In Daniel 10:19, "He said, "O man of high esteem, do not be afraid. Peace be with you; take courage and be courageous!" Now as soon as he spoke to me, I received strength and said, "May my lord speak, for you have strengthened me". Prayer in the waiting room is your defense against doubt and your sustainer in faith. When you pray, you will experience the courage needed to wait and the courage needed to act. While in the waiting room, set your mind on the promises of God.

In the Bible, the followers of God remained in waiting rooms. Daniel waited twenty-one days for an answer from the Lord, David waited fifteen years to be king, and the people of

God waited many years for the birth of Jesus. If they waited with expectation and faith, so can you. In the spiritual waiting room, we need to pray and persevere daily. In addition, we must prepare for God's answer. In a physical waiting room, there are magazines, advertisements, and pamphlets that give you information about your current situation or how to prepare for a future issue. In the same way, ask the Lord to show you how to prepare for His answer. Maybe it's a better understanding of how grace helps you during suffering or how to remain humble when exalted.

When I was in the early stages of my nerve pain, I read through the book of Job and numerous books about suffering by authors such as Joni Eareckson Tada and John Piper. I also read articles and medical information about my condition. I prayed and asked God to anchor me during those first years of pain. I didn't want to waver in my faith during the storm of health issues.

Further Bible Study

Look at the passages below and answer the following question: What does this passage of Scripture teach me about God and myself? Choose one passage of Scripture to anchor you this week.

1. 1 Samuel 1 – look at Hannah in the waiting room

2. Genesis 16–18 – look at Abraham and Sarah in the waiting room

3. Psalm 27:14

4. Psalm 33:20

5. Psalm 40:1

6. Romans 8:25

Reflection Questions

1. Do you have a hard time waiting for God to answer?

2. What could you do to increase your patience while you wait?

3. What has God taught you about waiting?

4. What are you waiting for now?

10

AnchoredinPrayer

Prayer can be described as the chain that connects the

anchor to the ship. We use our minds to pray, think about
God's goodness, memorize His Word, and try to process our
situations.

What is the focus of your prayers? How often do you
pray? Are you praying to the God of the Bible? These are
questions we could all ask ourselves.

In 1 Thessalonians 5:17, we read, "pray without ceasing".
In verses 12–28, Paul challenges the church of Thessalonica to
live as if they belong to Christ. We see in the gospels, especially
in the book of Luke, that Jesus had a reputation for praying.
He often slipped away to pray (Luke 5:16). What is my
reputation regarding prayer?

If the Word of God says to pray without ceasing, then I
should be praying about everything, from the time I wake up to
the time I go to sleep. It should be a foundation and driving
force in my life. It is what comforts me in my afflictions, it is

what I do to celebrate, it is what I do to make decisions, and it is what I do to gain strength for the day.

Being anchored in prayer means prayer is your default, the compass that leads you to peace. It is one of the main characteristics of a follower of Christ. Prayer started in Jesus' life with His mother in Luke 1:46–56. Mary begins by exalting the Lord and recalling the truths about God that she learned as a young girl. When the Lord does a miraculous thing in your life, does it make you remember His faithfulness over the years?

This passage shows that Mary was a follower of God

before she became pregnant with Jesus. She remembers God's mercy, His blessings, His mighty deeds, His victories over nations, His care for the hungry, and His promise of a Messiah. Mary speaks about the goodness of God because those truths are filling her mind. We see proof of a young woman who has prayed, studied the scrolls, and remembered the truths about God. In Luke 2, we read that Anna, the prophetess, and Simeon prayed for the redemption of Jerusalem through the birth of the promised Messiah. When they finally saw Christ face to face, they knew that their prayers had been answered.

If we are to pray without ceasing, then prayer is needed in every area of our lives and can be utilized in every situation we encounter. One way to understand prayer is to use the word as an acronym.

Here is one example.

P – pouring

R – requests

A – acknowledge

Y – yielding of the flesh

E – every situation

R – reverence

Pouring

Prayer is your soul and heart speaking to the Father, Son, and Holy Spirit. In Psalm 27:7–8, the Psalmist asks the Lord to hear his cry and answer him. Pouring out is getting to the point of boldness and humility in your prayer where you are crying out literally or figuratively. You are laying it all out before the Lord. In verse 8, the Psalmist reminds the Lord that He asks us to seek His face and responds that he is obedient by seeking the Lord with his heart. When we pray to the Lord, it comes from our hearts. We are telling the Lord everything from our fears, excitement, frustrations, and concerns. Our prayers may be with words or groaning or just our tears. Romans 12:8 says the Holy Spirit can discern our requests and give them to the Father.

Think about Hannah in 1 Samuel chapter 1. We meet her during the yearly time of worship. Her heart and soul are in so much anguish she cannot eat and is looking downcast at the table. The other wife of Elkanah is taunting her because, to date, she has been unable to bear children. Her husband thinks, "I'll console her by telling her to be grateful that she has me as a husband and that I'm better than ten sons" (1 Samuel 1:8

paraphrased). This statement makes me shake my head and say, "You just don't get it, Elkanah." Hannah musters up some energy and eats and drinks while with her husband, but she is still in turmoil in her heart. She then goes to the temple alone and weeps bitterly before the Lord. Her relationship with the Lord invites her to go to Him and cry out to Him.

It's hard when people don't allow you the space and time to grieve, but rather, they want you to get over it like Hannah's husband did. In those times, you must get away, pray to your Father, and pour it all out before Him. In verses 10–13, we see Hannah pouring everything out to God. There are no words, but her lips are moving. The words are coming from her heart and are being conveyed through the Holy Spirit to the Father. As the priest, Eli, watches her, he thinks she is drunk and confronts her, but this is where you see the strength prayer has just granted Hannah. We see her response in 1 Samuel 1:15: "But Hannah replied, "No, my lord, I am a woman oppressed in spirit; I have drunk neither wine nor strong drink, but I have poured out my soul before the Lord". We must be vulnerable, like Hannah, before the Lord and pour out our souls to Him.

Requests

To request means to let God know what you want. Two passages will help us understand this part of prayer: Job 6:8 and Philippians 4:6. In these two passages, we see the words requests, supplication, or petition in various translations. Job hopes the Lord will listen and grant him what he has requested, while Paul encourages the saints to pray and implore the Lord for their concerns. When we pray, we are requesting, not commanding, God to answer us. Sometimes we can come to view our requests as a debit card that we put in the automated teller machine (ATM) called God. When we think like this, we say, "God give me exactly what I asked for in the way I want it," and treat God like a genie. In Ecclesiastes 5:2, Solomon reminds us of our position, "Do not be hasty in word or impulsive in thought to bring up a matter in the presence of God. For God is in heaven and you are on the earth; therefore let your words be few".

Humility must cover our requests. We aren't coming to God fearfully but humbly and asking Him to answer us. Remember that you are a child of God—He is your father, and He will not get tired of hearing or answering your multiple requests. Unlike with our earthly fathers, we can ask Him the same request repeatedly. He wants to hear our hearts. He wants us to cry out to Him.

Acknowledge

Remember, in the chapter about being anchored in the waiting room, I stated that we must pray daily. Consistent and confident prayer is only possible when you know that the God you are praying to is more than capable of dealing with your situation. In my office at work, I have a large poster on my wall with the heading, "And He Shall Be Called." The poster lists all the names given to Christ in the Bible. When I look at this list of names, I recall that there is a story behind each one. These names show the character of Christ, whether He is the bread of life or the good shepherd. In John, the Lord Jesus states who He is by sharing seven I AM statements. These are comforting to me because they unite Jesus Christ with the God who revealed Himself as "I AM" to Moses in Exodus 3:14.

John 6:35, 41, 48, 51	**I am the bread of life.**
John 8:12	**I am the light of the world.**
John 10:7, 9	**I am the door of the sheep.**
John 10:11, 14	**I am the good shepherd.**
John 11:25	**I am the resurrection and the life.**
John 14:6	**I am the way, the truth, and the life.**
John 15:1, 5	**I am the true vine.**

Take a moment to reflect deeply on one of these and focus on how believing this truth about Christ will help you develop an anchored mindset.

In John 6, Jesus states that He is the bread of life four times. Our bodies need physical nourishment, but our spirits also need nourishment, which Christ refers to as the bread of life. Think about the prophet Elijah when he was on the run from Jezebel in 1 Kings 19. While in the wilderness and asking God to let him die, he fell asleep. When he awoke, there was a bread cake baking on hot stones before him. The angel spoke to him and told him to eat because the journey was too grueling for him. He ate portions of that bread cake twice and had enough energy for forty days and forty nights. This passage shows that the Lord uses bread to give man strength for his journey.

In the story of the Israelites' exodus from Egypt, God commanded the people to remember His deliverance by observing the Feast of Unleavened Bread. They didn't have time to allow the bread to rise because God would deliver them quickly. I believe that every time they ate unleavened bread, they spoke about the deliverance God had given them. In Deuteronomy chapter 8, Moses took the time to remind the new generation of how God had taught them over the past forty years.

"He humbled you and let you be hungry, and fed you with manna which you did not know, nor did your fathers know, that He might make you understand that man does not live by bread alone, but man lives by everything that proceeds out of the mouth of the LORD"(Deuteronomy 8:3)

Please think about these three words used in Deuteronomy 8:3: humbled, hungry, and fed. We are supposed to be able to work and provide food, shelter, and clothing for ourselves, but when you cannot do that for various reasons, it will humble you. In that state of humility, you will be tempted to do anything to get bread. Think of the story of Esau and Jacob. Esau is so hungry that he trades his birthright for food. Then compare that story with Jesus being tempted by Satan while in the wilderness. In Luke 4:3, Satan tempts Jesus to turn a stone into bread because he has been without food for forty days and is hungry. Our Savior doesn't fall for the temptation and instead quotes Deuteronomy 8:3 because Jesus knows we will need to see this example. He didn't need the bread because the task of obeying His Father was His food. The words of His Father fed him for those forty days.

Let's decide to feast on the Lord and ask Him to fill us with the desire to obey. If you have ever chosen to fast from food for spiritual direction from the Lord, then you have experienced the temptation to eat before the fast is complete. I would encourage you to feast on God's word when you choose to fast from eating if it will not negatively affect your health. Let the Word of God be your meal. Take a moment to acknowledge the Savior who feeds and sustains you for the journey before you. Jesus is the good shepherd, and he will make sure you have what you need in every season of your life.

Yearning for the Lord

When we pray, we choose not to rely on our flesh or others to meet our needs. Instead, we submit our needs to the Father. Psalm 63:1 reads, "O God, You are my God; I shall seek You earnestly; My soul thirsts for You, my flesh yearns for You, In a dry and weary land where there is no water". Some synonyms for yearns are craves, desires, and hungers. When we pray, our mind, body, and soul must crave to hear a word from the Lord in the same way a dehydrated person craves water.

When you pray, you first acknowledge that there is only one God and He is the one who made heaven and earth and has forgiven you of your sins through the resurrection of Christ. You are seeking Him with your heart, soul, and mind. Remember, in the chapter on why we need an anchor, I asked you to think of your soul as the ship that must be anchored to Christ. Your soul is where your thirst and hunger for the Lord reside. Your soul is where you experience anguish and comfort. Your soul is where you experience depression and deliverance. Your soul is where you rest in the grace granted to you. When your soul is thirsting for the Lord, your body will also yearn for the Lord. Your body will desire to have God always present, and you will not be satisfied or content with anything else.

Every Situation

Paul instructs believers always to pray and not stop praying (1 Thessalonians 5:17, paraphrased). As believers, we are often asked the question, "Did you pray about *it*?" or someone tells us, "You need to pray about *that* first." I believe we say these things because "it and that" are significant situations that may have weighty consequences if we choose incorrectly. Proverbs 11:14 states, "Where there is no guidance the people fall, But in abundance of counselors there is victory". Jesus is named the Wonderful Counselor in Isaiah 9:6. From whom better than Jesus could we possibly seek counsel? We can take every question to Him and are promised an answer.

As a new believer at age nineteen, I walked around the University of Illinois at Chicago campus with my small New Testament Bible. I would read as I walked to class and while sitting in my room. Whenever I had the time, I was reading. I often prayed about what to wear in the morning and which classes to register for each semester. I was building an intimate relationship with the Lord that has carried me through the most brutal storms in my life. There is nothing too small or too big to ask of the Lord. Psalm 138:8 states, "The Lord will accomplish what concerns me; Your lovingkindness, O LORD, is everlasting; Do not forsake the works of Your hands".

Reverence

We acknowledge that our prayers will be heard and answered by the Creator of the Universe, the God over all gods, the One who has no beginning or end. When we read how Christ taught the disciples to pray in Matthew 6:5–14, He reminds them that the Father knows what they need before they begin speaking. Fundamentally, Christ is teaching them that they are speaking to one who isn't dependent on the way they speak, the posture they have when praying, or how many words they use because He already knows their hearts. Reverence for God begins when you focus on the One you are praying to, rather than how you are praying. The reverence you have for the Father is not the reverence you have for a king you don't know. Instead, you have respect and honor for the one who has given you eternal life. An earthly king can't know you spiritually, physically, and mentally, but your Father in heaven knows exactly what you need. Our Father is above all rule and authority and can see all things because of who He is.

As the Psalmist says in Psalm 139:7–8, we will never be out of His presence. He is the most attentive Father we could ever have. When we think about His character as the perfect Father to us, that should cause us to treat Him with the utmost respect.

May you be anchored in prayer, knowing that your prayers are not falling on deaf ears but rather are heard by the Holy Spirit and taken directly to your Father in heaven.

Further Bible Study

Look at the passages below and answer the following question: What does this passage of Scripture teach me about God and myself? Choose one passage of Scripture to anchor you this week.

1. Psalm 66:17–20

2. Romans 8:26

3. Hebrews 7:25

4. Hebrews 8:1-2

5. I John 5:15

Reflection Questions

1. Considering the mnemonic device for prayer. Does this help you understand prayer?

2. When was the last time you prayed for forgiveness?

3. What do you need to pour out before the Lord in prayer?

4. Do you have faith that God the Father will answer your prayers?

11

11

Anchored

Anchored

I wanted to take some time to give an overall description of acronym below, and each chapter you've read fits into this breakdown.

A – All of us encounter storms.

N – Never lean on your understanding.

C – Can't depend on the strength of others.

H – Hope in Christ and Christ alone.

O – Obey what God has written and revealed to you.

R – Rest in the fact that Christ has the power to calm the storm.

In this final chapter, I want to discuss the type of anchor Christ is, delve into Hebrews 6:19, and explore how we live this out daily.

Anchors are divided into two categories, temporary and permanent. A temporary anchor is the most common type of anchor. It can stabilize a ship amid a storm, hold it close to the shore, and comes in different shapes and sizes. According to *The Complete Anchoring Handbook,* there are ten temporary anchor categories.19 They are: classic stock anchors, modified stock anchors, pivoting stockless anchors, CQR anchors, pivoting-fluke stock anchors, lightweight anchors, claw anchors, plow anchors, concave fluke anchors, and roll bar anchors. I bet you thought there was only one type of anchor because of the tattoo on Popeye the Sailor's arm. I know I just aged myself with that reference to Popeye, but that was one of my favorite cartoons growing up. It's funny how God has been putting anchors in my view from an early age. The anchor on Popeye's arm is the fisherman's anchor, which falls into the category of classic stock anchors.

Each of these temporary anchors is fitted and tested to work with various seabeds and various sizes of boats. The claw anchors come in various types, one of which is the SuperMAX rigid anchor. This anchor penetrates and holds very well, and when the wind or current changes direction, it realigns itself readily without drifting or losing its hold. This anchor reminds me of Christ. He can penetrate heaven and hold exceptionally well to God's promises. When the trial or tribulation seeks to capsize us, He realigns and holds us.

Yes, Jesus is our SuperMAX rigid anchor. When He realigns, He uses the Spirit of God to remind us of who He is and who we are. Instead of saying we are a failure, we remember that we are victorious. Christ is our temporary anchor because we currently reside as strangers. Earth is not

---

[19] Alain Poiraud, *The Complete Anchoring Handbook: Stay Put On Any Bottom In Any Weather. (9780071475082)* (Blacklick, Ohio: McGraw-Hill, 2008), 19-23.

our home forever. Jesus stays with us to sustain us throughout our lives.

There are two characteristics of an anchor: its design and holding power. Well, the same is true for our anchor, Christ. His two characteristics are grace and truth. The design of the anchor determines when and where it can be utilized to stabilize a ship. Compared to this, Jesus gives us grace when we are convicted of sin by the Holy Spirit, so we can still have hope. His grace is that we can be forgiven. Jesus gives us grace when we are going through a hardship by reminding us that He, too, endured hardships and persevered to the end. Jesus gives us grace when we are stressed by life's concerns, providing peace through prayer about the situation as stated in Philippians 4:6–7. In every situation, the grace of Jesus is needed and used to anchor our souls, keeping us from being anxious.

The holding power of an anchor is the strength it must possess to hold a boat in various conditions encountered at sea. In our key passage, Luke 8:22–25, Jesus showed His power to hold the minds of the disciples. The disciples, like us, had become anxious that they would die; they began to doubt that Jesus cared about them. But when they called on His name, He quickly calmed the storm, which inevitably brought them to a point of revelation that Jesus could be completely trusted. Please don't miss this vital point: what you believe about Jesus will directly affect how anxious you get in various situations. If you have believed that every word spoken of Him in Scripture is true and you have surrendered your life to Him, then you have hope. That hope leads you to believe that God has first approved every single trial and tribulation in your life, and you know that the Father, Son, and Holy Spirit are all working to ensure that you will make it through.

Jesus is the truth and spoke the truth that is His holding power. In every situation He encountered, whether it was being tempted by Satan, being questioned by doubters, or being accused of lying by the religious leaders, He always responded with truth. He often reminded them of the prophecies made about Him and the miracles He had performed.

Additionally, all anchors must undergo rigorous tests and securely hold to one or more types of seabeds. These seabeds are divided into sand, mud, gravel, and rocks. Think of seabeds as circumstances in our lives.

We can liken sand to the times when things keep changing. We feel as if we finally have our footing, but at that moment, something else happens. In these times, Jesus reminds us in Hebrews 13:8 that He is the same yesterday, today, and forever. During those changing times, I can remain connected and dependent upon my anchor, Christ, who never changes.

Mud is like temptation because we can become stuck in it and unsure of how to free ourselves. Christ tells us in 1 Corinthians 10:13 that He will always give us a way out of our temptation, and in Psalm 40:2, He will lift us from the mud.

Gravel is the hardest sediment in which to anchor because gravel shifts, and there isn't any cohesion. Gravel can be compared to the heart of doubting followers of Christ. They constantly waver between trusting Him and doubting Him. They blame Christ for not providing security for them, but they lack faith in Christ. Their faith isn't secure. It is hard to minister to someone like this because they want proof that God will secure them *before* they trust Him. I would compare them to the followers of Christ who came to see the signs and wonders but weren't committed to Him.

Lastly, rock represents seasons when things are hard and seem impossible. Christ tells us in Matthew 19:26 that nothing is impossible for the Lord.

Now let's look at Hebrews 6:18–19:

So that by two unchangeable things (*God's promise/His word and God's oath/His character*) which it is impossible for God to lie, we who have taken refuge (*the one we run to*) would have strong encouragement (*assurance that we will have hope*) to take hold of the hope (*Jesus*) set before us. This hope (*Jesus*) we have as an anchor (*temporary*) of the soul (*our security/safety*), a hope (*Jesus*) both sure and steadfast (*can be depended on*) and one which enters within the veil (*takes us to the Father*) (interpretations mine).

Remember, I spoke of Jesus as our anchor having two characteristics: grace and truth. Those two characteristics of Christ won't change because we can depend upon the Word of God that said those things about Him and the character of God. We talked about God's promise to Abraham in Genesis 15 to make him a father of many descendants and how the Lord followed up with a covenant between them. God has also promised He would give us eternal life and sealed that promise with an oath through the blood of Christ. We run to this hope just like people convicted of murder ran to the cities of refuge in Old Testament times. We find security and safety in Christ. Our SuperMAX rigid anchor assures us of this in Ephesians 1:13–14: "In Him, you also, after listening to the message of truth, the gospel of your salvation—having also believed, you were sealed in Him with the Holy Spirit of promise, who is given as a pledge of our inheritance, with a view to the redemption of God's own possession to the praise of His glory".

Jesus is not going to leave or forsake you. He made a promise to you and sealed that promise with His blood. You can rest in the fact that you are secure with Him. Do you want to take a deep breath and rest in Him? Are you tired of going to ineffective anchors that don't give you security? Hebrews 6:18 states that hope is set before us. Jesus, the Good Shepherd, is leading you, and you are His sheep. Keeping your eyes fixed on the Shepherd gives you hope, listening to the Shepherd's voice gives you direction, and learning from the experiences of the Shepherd gives you wisdom. Trusting in Him makes you wise and allows you to reach the right
decisions amid trials or temptations.

Jesus is our SuperMAX rigid anchor for our soul. In *The MacArthur New Testament Commentary of Hebrews* he states, "As our High Priest, Jesus serves as the anchor of our souls, the One who will forever keep us from drifting away from God."20 Your hardships are the storm, and your soul is the ship. Your soul is where all your desires and emotions reside. Our souls can rejoice, be downcast, seek God, and rest in God. It is the part of us that must be anchored, or we will capsize.

In *The NIV Study Bible*, the commentary for the words as an anchor for the soul in Hebrews 6:19 reads, "Like an anchor holding a ship safely in position, our hope in Christ guarantees our safety. Whereas the ship's anchor goes down to the ocean bed, the Christian's anchor goes up into the true, heavenly sanctuary, where he is moored to God himself."21 We must look to our anchor, Christ, because He sets our hearts, minds, and souls to what is eternal. These earth issues feel

---

[20] John MacArthur, *The MacArthur New Testament Commentary: Hebrews* (Chicago, Illinois: Moody, 1983), 168.
[21] *The NIV Study Bible*, 10th ed. (Grand Rapids, Michigan: Zondervan, 1995), 1864.

insurmountable but are just a dot in eternity. Think about the ocean's vastness as eternity and our time on earth like throwing a pebble into the ocean. We will spend eternity with the Lord, never to deal with temptation or hardships again.

That is the hope that Christ gives us. He links us to the Father in Hebrews 7:25, "Therefore, He is able to also save forever those who draw near to God through Him, since He always lives to make intercession for them".

Jesus is eternal, and He has direct access to the Father. He is working on your behalf right now; He wants to steady you. I want you to imagine and draw this image in the margin. A ship with a chain that is going up to heaven, the anchor is sitting on a throne. The ship is our soul, and our mind is the chain anchored to Christ on His throne in heaven.

The question now is how to live an anchored life with Christ. The first step is acknowledging that your soul can be shaken if not connected to an anchor. A ship has a primary and a secondary anchor, which steps in if the primary anchor fails. Christ must be your primary and secondary. He settles you in every situation you encounter on earth, and when this earth is no more or you leave this earth, He has you already anchored to heaven, which will be your eternal home.

One of my favorite hymns is "Come Thou Fount of Every Blessing." The third verse says, "Let thy goodness, like a fetter, bind my wandering heart to Thee. Prone to wander, Lord, I feel it, prone to leave the God I love; Here's my heart, O take and seal it, Seal it for Thy courts above."22

The second step is to acknowledge that your soul will hope in something whether it's people, itself, or Christ. The

---

22 Thomas, J. H. *Come, Thou Fount of Every Blessing.* Catskill: Thomas, J. H, 1872. Notated Music. Retrieved from the Library of Congress, <www.loc.gov/item/2023816798/>.

third step is to ask with every tribulation, "Where is my faith?" The fourth step is you must stand firm and answer the question by stating that your faith is not in an ineffective anchor, which is you or another person, a viewpoint, a denomination, or a political party. All of those are ineffective anchors and will leave you feeling insecure and vulnerable to the effects of the tribulation. The fifth step is we proclaim amid the storm—when you get the call, when you see the destruction of a city, when you lose a loved one, when you are disgusted with the evil in the world—that *Christ alone is your anchor*! Lastly, you remember the end of the story is eternity with Christ and the fellow seamen/sea women who have weathered the storms of life and are receiving the crown of life. James 1:12 states, "Blessed is a man who perseveres under trial; for once he has been approved, he will receive the crown of life which the Lord has promised to those who love Him".

No one else can make that promise to us!
Revelation 2:10 states, "Do not fear what you are about to suffer. Behold, the devil is about to cast some of you into prison, so that you will be tested, and you will have tribulation for ten days. Be faithful until death, and I will give you the crown of life".

In both passages, God encourages us to persevere or be faithful. We are adopting a new belief system that says *Lord Jesus, I will accept you as my primary and secondary anchor*. We must decide before the tribulation comes to make Christ our anchor.

Have you made Him your anchor? Have you accepted His gift of salvation? Have you confessed with your mouth and believed in your heart that Christ has been raised from the dead? Please don't assume you are saved but be assured of your salvation. I want to know that your soul is anchored in the Lord. This anchor only holds those that belong to Him.

Further Bible Study:

Look at the passages below and answer the following question: What does this passage of Scripture teach me about God and myself? I am giving you twelve passages to study through each month for a year if you accept this challenge.

1. Hebrews 6:19

2. Matthew 5:3–12

3. Romans 5

4. Romans 12:1–2

5. Philippians 1:6; 2:3; 3:8; 4:4

6. Joshua 24:14–15

7. Exodus 20:1–17

8. Matthew 22:37–40

9. Ephesians 6:10–18

10. Psalm 100:1–5

11. John 1:1–4; 12–14

12. Revelation 19:7–8, 11-16

Reflection Questions

1. Are you viewing Christ as a SuperMAX rigid anchor?

2. Is Christ your primary and secondary anchor?

3. What type of seabed are you in currently? Sand, mud, gravel, or rocks?

4. What have you been hoping in/for if not Christ?

5. Have you seen the difference between hoping in Christ or hoping in someone else amid your tribulations?

6. What has the Lord taught you while reading this book?

Conclusion

I pray the Lord has met you while you read these eleven

chapters. I hope God challenged you to look at your faith keenly. I would not be surprised if some of you experienced a storm while reading this book. We can't be satisfied with allowing worry and anxiety to come into our lives when the storm arrives. We must be believers who accept Christ as our anchor and remind ourselves that this earth is not our home.

In these chapters, I discussed how to identify a storm and its three key characteristics. First, it is out of your control; second, it's beyond your comprehension; and third, it's not manageable by your mental or physical strength. When going through the storm, keep your mind fixed on the end goal of following Christ. The disciples followed Christ by getting into the boat and traveling to the other side of the Sea of Galilee. They didn't know the storm was coming, nor do we. We do know that Christ allows the storm, He ordains how long the storm will last, and He will stop the storm.

Christ has the power to sustain you. Your only job is to believe He is powerful enough to comfort you during the storm.

Take the time to look through the Word of God and put the symbol of a fisherman's anchor next to the passages that give you comfort amid a storm. I encourage you to memorize them and recite them as often as possible. The Word of God has the power to revive and refresh you, as stated in Psalm 19:7–8: "The law of the LORD is perfect, restoring the soul; the testimony of the LORD is sure, making wise the simple. The precepts of the LORD are right, rejoicing the heart; The commandment of the LORD is pure, enlightening the eyes".

You can't experience this type of rejuvenation without the Word of God. Those ineffective anchors we discussed earlier in the book may give you a quick fix, but they cannot provide peace, joy, and clarity of mind.

You have a choice to make today. Will you be anxious or anchored? Anxiety will steal your happiness, cause double-mindedness, and blind you from seeing the hand of God. God has given us clear commandments in Scripture regarding anxiety. He has told us not to be anxious but pray about everything. The anchored mind begins with prayer. Pray before, during, and after the storm. After the storm, say a prayer of thanksgiving and ask God to prepare you to be a witness of His goodness. People will go through a storm similar to the one you experienced, and they will need to know how to get through the storm. You will have an opportunity to share how James 1:2–4 became more than words on a page— instead, you experienced joy while in the trial because Christ is your anchor. "Consider it all joy, my brethren, when you encounter various trials, knowing that the testing of your faith produces endurance. And let endurance have its perfect result, so that you may be perfect and complete, lacking in nothing".

When Christ is your anchor, there is peace which brings joy and confidence with decisions, and you see even the most minor things God is doing amid the storm. Be anchored today, tomorrow, and until you see Christ face-to-face.

Appendix 1

Hopefully, God has spoken to you as you read this book.

Christ as Lord and Savior. Or maybe you want to share the gospel with the person reading this book with you.

There comes a time in every person's life when they need to stop and answer questions from God. Sit before the Lord and allow Him to ask you questions. I remember the day I sat still before the Lord, and He asked me, "Do you know what it means to be saved?" What questions has God been asking you? Maybe it's one of the following:

- "Do you believe in me?"
- "Do you trust me?"
- "Will you surrender your life to me?"

As believers, we repent. When God reveals His love for us, His power, and the authority He has over all humanity, it will cause us to repent.

The Gospel Presentation:

- God created the earth and made humans in His image.
  He commanded the first man and woman (Adam and Eve) not to eat from the tree of the knowledge of good

and evil. God promised that if they did eat from that tree they would die.

- Adam and Eve disobeyed God and ate from the tree of the knowledge of good and evil. The serpent tempted them with a lie that their eyes would be opened, they would be like God, and would know good and evil. The serpent also told them that they would not die.

- When Adam and Eve ate the fruit from the forbidden tree, they brought death to all humans. At that point they were made enemies of God because of their sin which was disobedience.

- Jesus is God in the flesh. He is the Son of God, and He came to give us eternal life by taking on the penalty of death.

- When we accept the gift of eternal life that came through Jesus Christ, we become children of God. To accept this gift, we must confess that we are sinners (have been and are disobedient to the commands of God) and repent of our sins.

If you are ready to become a child of God, take a few minutes and pray. You can begin like this,

Dear God, I confess that I have sinned against you, I believe that you are God and that you created me in your image. You loved me enough to send your Son Jesus Christ to die for my sins. Jesus, you took death for me, and I am thankful for your sacrifice. I repent of my sins and ask for forgiveness. I believe that Jesus Christ rose from the dead to give me eternal life. I pray to be saved from the penalty of sin in the name of Jesus Christ.

Amen

According to Romans 10:9–10 you are saved and now per Ephesians 2:13–14 you are sealed with the Holy Spirit. Now go and live the abundant life that has been given to you. Read the Word of God, study the Scriptures, pray, find a local body of believers to grow with and make disciples (Matthew 28:19–20).

About the Author

Ariyana grew up in the Chicagoland area. While in college, she saw the gospel lived out by two of her college friends, and not long after, she decided to follow Christ while visiting a church that met on her campus. She graduated from the University of Illinois at Chicago with a degree in kinesiology/sports medicine and worked as an athletic trainer and later completed her master's degree in social work from the University of Memphis. Ariyana moved to Memphis in 2008 to join the staff of Downline Ministries. She served as the women's director for the Emerging Leaders program for six years. She states those years shaped her heart for discipleship as she poured into women.

While on staff at Downline Ministries, she began volunteering with Moriah House, the women's recovery program of Memphis Union Mission. She began teaching Bible lessons to the ladies and soon discovered her love for women in these situations. She was offered a counselor position in 2014, and in 2018, she became the executive director of Moriah House. She has seen the importance of discipleship in the lives of the women she counsels at Moriah House. In January of 2024, she began working for her church, Fellowship Memphis, as the Care Ministry Director and Business Administrator.

She began raising her cousin Zion in 2016, and through much prayer and guidance from the Holy Spirit, she decided to adopt her in 2022. Parenting is the most challenging yet most fulfilling aspect of her life. In addition to parenting, she teaches at her church, conferences locally and internationally, and at the Downline Institute. Her passion for discipleship and the Word of God is contagious. She desires to help people approach the trials of life through the study of God's Word.

Contact Ariyana:

Email: ariyana@beanchoredtochrist.org

www.ingramcontent.com/pod-product-compliance
Lightning Source LLC
Chambersburg PA
CBHW071521120626
46550CB00006B/2303